Trend Houses
Exemplifying a Variety of Distinctive Living Patterns

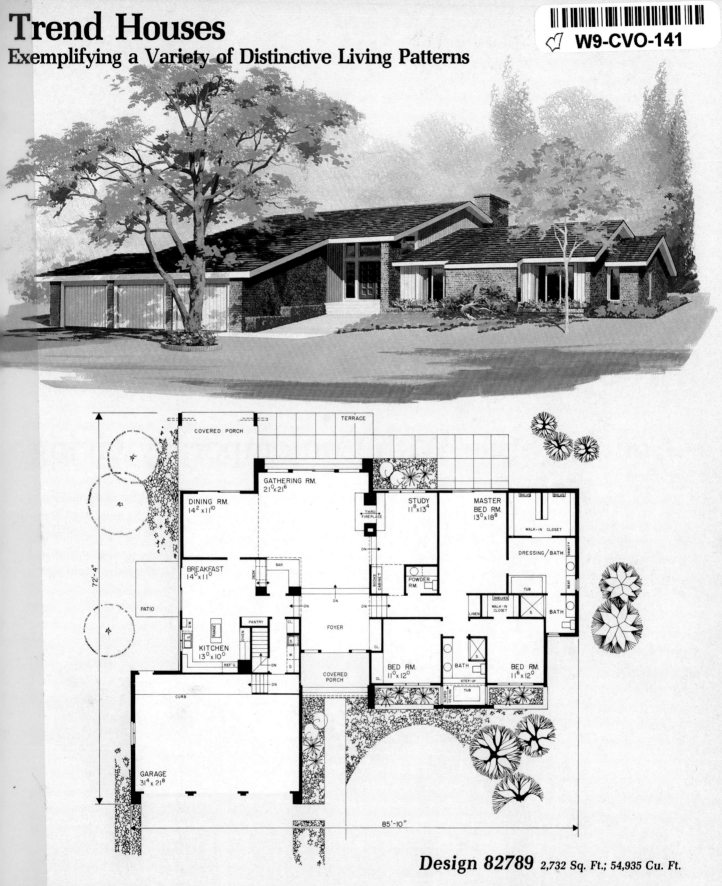

Design 82789 2,732 Sq. Ft.; 54,935 Cu. Ft.

● Dramatic contemporary styling is apparent in this impressive one-story design. This home has exceptional livability as one will immediately observe by going through the double front doors. Inside, a foyer greets all visitors and leads them to each of the three areas, each down a few steps. Straight ahead, the living area has a large gathering room with a fireplace. A study is adjacent on one side while the formal dining room is on the other. The work center to the left has an efficient kitchen with an island range, breakfast room, laundry and built-in desk and bar. The three bedroom sleeping area is to the right of the foyer. Excellent bath facilities throughout.

Country Style With Contemporary Living

● A country-style home is part of America's fascination with the rural past. This home's emphasis of the traditional country home is in its historic gambrel roof, dormers and fanlight windows. Having a traditional exterior from the street view, this two-story home has large window walls and a greenhouse, which opens the house to the outdoors in a thoroughly contemporary manner. The interior of this design was planned to meet the requirements of today's active family. Like the country houses of the past, this home has a large gathering room for family get-togethers or entertaining. Note its L-shape which accommodates a music alcove. This area is large enough for a grand piano and storage for TV/Stereo equipment.

Design 82883

1,919 Sq. Ft. - First Floor
895 Sq. Ft. - Second Floor; 46,489 Cu. Ft.

The adjacent two-story greenhouse doubles as the dining room. There is a pass-thru snack bar to the country kitchen here. This country kitchen just might be the heart of the house with its two areas - the work zone and the sitting room. A front study is ready for those more quiet retreats.

There are four bedrooms on the two floors - the master bedroom suite on the first floor; and three more on the second floor. A lounge, overlooking the gathering room and front foyer, is also on the second floor. The greenhouse adds 140 sq. ft. and 2,170 cu. ft. to the figures quoted above.

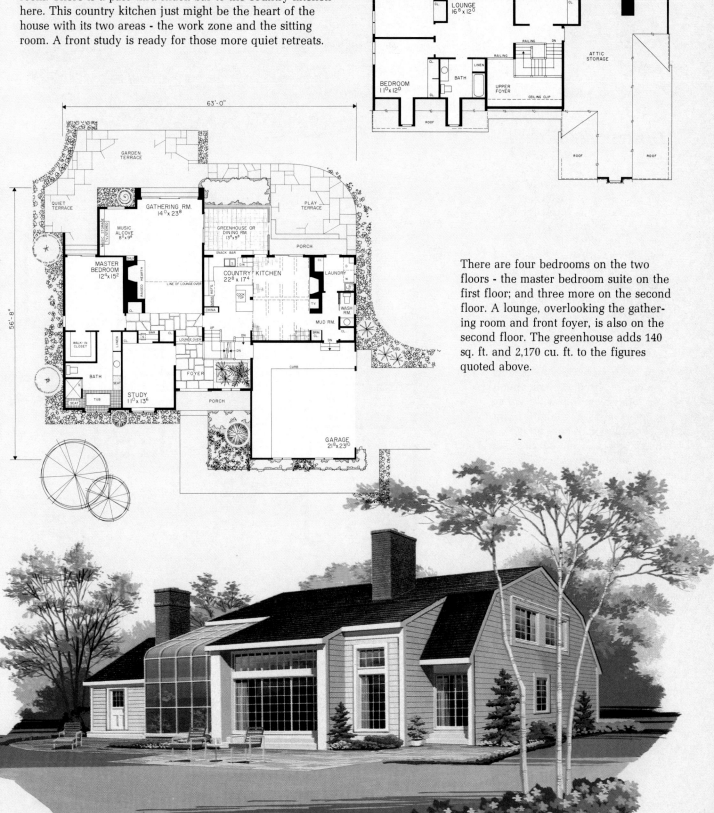

Design 82857

2,982 Sq. Ft.; 60,930 Cu. Ft.

● Imagine yourself occupying this home! Study the outstanding master bedroom. You will be forever pleased by its many features. It has "his" and "her" baths each with a large walk-in closet, sliding glass doors to a private, side terrace (a great place to enjoy a morning cup of coffee) and an adjacent study. Notice that the two family bedrooms are separated from the master bedroom. This allows for total privacy both for the parents and the children. Continue to observe this plan. You will have no problem at all entertaining in the gathering room. Your party can flow to the adjacent balcony on a warm summer evening. The work center has been designed in an orderly fashion. The U-shaped kitchen utilizes the triangular work pattern, said to be the most efficient. Only a few steps away, you will be in the breakfast room, formal dining room, laundry or wash room. Take your time and study every last detail in this home plan.

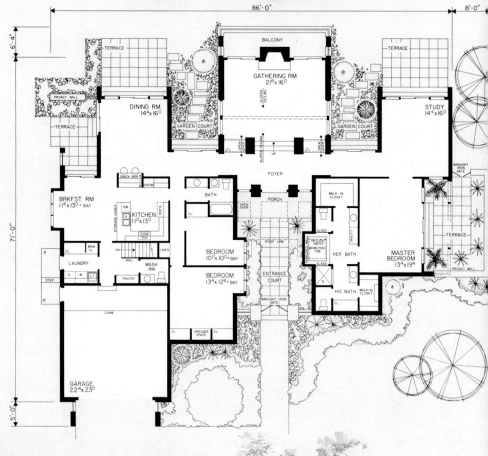

Design 82909 1,221 Sq. Ft. - First Floor
767 Sq. Ft. - Second Floor; 38,954 Cu. Ft.

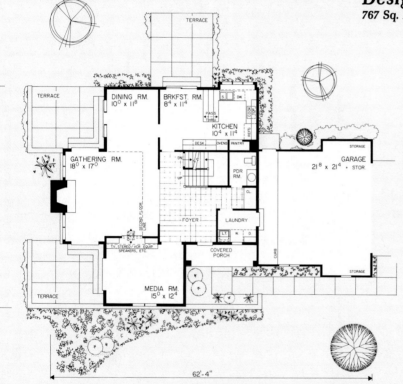

● This charming traditional home with striking good looks offers the modern family plenty of contemporary amenities. The first floor features a large gathering room with fireplace, media room for stereos and VCRs, a convenient kitchen with breakfast room, plus a dining room. The second floor includes an upper gathering room, spacious master bedroom suite, and a second bedroom. Notice columns that support a covered porch and window treatments.

This attractive, contemporary bi-level will overwhelm you with its features: two balconies, an open staircase with planter below, two lower level bedrooms, six sets of sliding glass doors and an outstanding master suite loaded with features. The occupants of this house will love the large exercise room. After a tough workout, you can relax in the whirlpool or the sauna or simply take a shower!

Design 82856 1,801 Sq. Ft. - Upper Level
2,170 Sq. Ft. - Lower Level; 44,934 Cu. Ft.

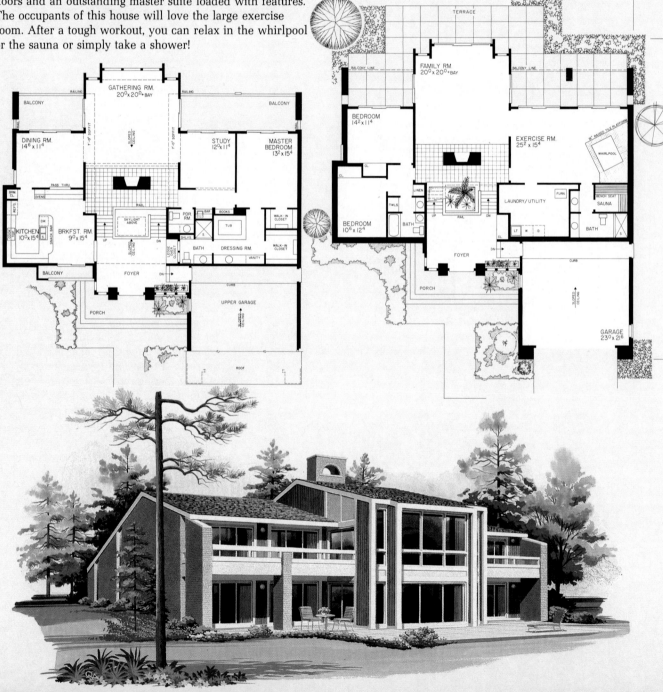

● This contemporary, hillside home is very inviting. A large kitchen with an adjacent snack bar makes light meals a breeze. The adjoining breakfast room offers a scenic view through sliding glass doors. Notice the sloped ceiling in the dining and gathering rooms. A fireplace in the gathering room adds a cozy air. An interesting feature is the master bedroom's easy access to the study. Also, take note of the sliding doors in the master bedroom which lead to a private balcony. On the lower level, a large activities room will be a frequently used spot by family members. The fireplace and wet bar add a nice touch for entertaining friends. Take note of the two or optional three bedrooms - the choice is yours. Obviously, this house offers lots of livability and will be a joy to own.

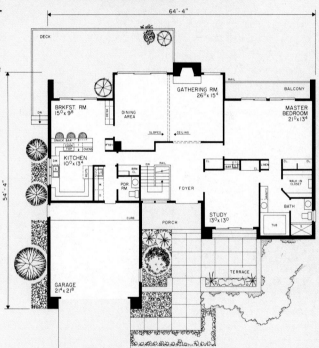

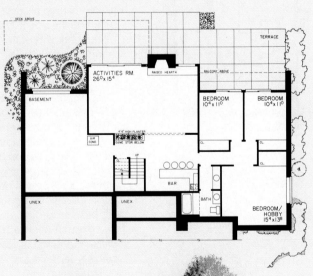

Design 82896 1,856 Sq. Ft. - **Main Level**
1,454 Sq. Ft. - **Lower Level**; 43,390 Cu. Ft.

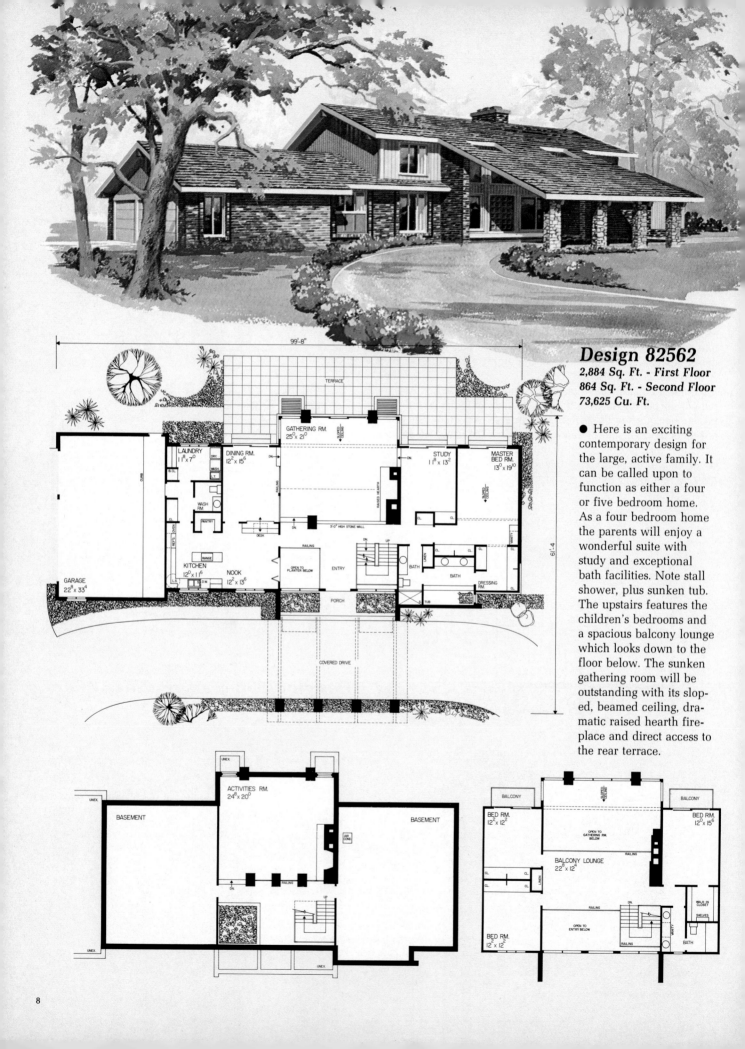

Design 82562

2,884 Sq. Ft. - First Floor
864 Sq. Ft. - Second Floor
73,625 Cu. Ft.

● Here is an exciting contemporary design for the large, active family. It can be called upon to function as either a four or five bedroom home. As a four bedroom home the parents will enjoy a wonderful suite with study and exceptional bath facilities. Note stall shower, plus sunken tub. The upstairs features the children's bedrooms and a spacious balcony lounge which looks down to the floor below. The sunken gathering room will be outstanding with its sloped, beamed ceiling, dramatic raised hearth fireplace and direct access to the rear terrace.

99'-8"

TERRACE

GATHERING RM.
25⁰ x 21⁰

SLOPED CEILING

STUDY
11⁸ x 13²

MASTER BED RM.
13⁰ x 19¹⁰

SLOPED CEILING

LAUNDRY
11⁸ x 7⁰

DINING RM.
12² x 15⁶

WASH RM.

PANTRY

RAISED HEARTH

3'-0" HIGH STONE WALL

CL

CL

VANITY

DRESSING RM.

KITCHEN
12⁰ x 11⁶

RANGE

NOOK
12² x 13⁶

DESK

OPEN TO PLANTER BELOW

RAILING

ENTRY

DN

UP

BATH

LINEN

CL

CL

BATH

CL

GARAGE
22⁸ x 33⁴

PORCH

TUB

61'-4"

COVERED DRIVE

Basement

UNEX.

BASEMENT

ACTIVITIES RM.
24⁸ x 20⁰

BASEMENT

AIR COND.

RAILING

UNEX.

UNEX.

DN.

UP

UNEX.

Second Floor

BALCONY

BED RM.
12² x 12²

SLOPED CEILING

BALCONY

BED RM.
12⁰ x 15⁶

OPEN TO GATHERING RM. BELOW

RAILING

BALCONY LOUNGE
22⁸ x 12⁴

CL

CL

LINEN

WALK-IN CLOSET

SHELVES

BED RM.
12² x 12²

OPEN TO ENTRY BELOW

RAILING

DN.

VANITY

BATH

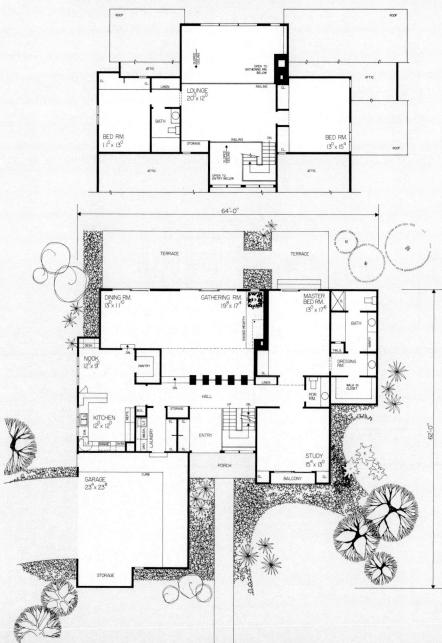

Design 82708
2,108 Sq. Ft. - First Floor
824 Sq. Ft. - Second Floor
52,170 Cu. Ft.

● Here is a one-and-a-half story home whose exterior is distinctive. It has a contemporary feeling, yet it retains some of the fine design features and proportions of traditional exteriors. Inside the appealing double front doors, there is livability galore. The sunken rear living-dining area is delightfully spacious and is looked down into from the second floor lounge. The open end fireplace with its raised hearth and planter is another focal point. The master bedroom features a fine compartmented bath with both shower and tub. The study is just a couple steps away. The U-shaped kitchen is outstanding. Notice the pantry and laundry. Upstairs provides children with their own sleeping, studying and TV quarters. Absolutely a great design! Study all of the fine details closely with your family.

Clutter Room, Media Room To The Fore

● Something new? Something new, indeed!! Here is the introduction of two rooms which will make a wonderful contribution to family living. The clutter room is strategically placed between the kitchen and garage. It is the nerve center of the work area. It houses the laundry, provides space for sewing, has a large sorting table, and even plenty of space for the family's tool bench. A handy potting area is next to the laundry tray. Adjacent to the clutter room, and a significant part of the planning of this whole zone, are the pantry and freezer with their nearby counter space. These facilities surely will expedite the unloading of groceries from the car and their convenient storing. Wardrobe and broom closets, plus washroom complete the outstanding utility of this area. The location of the clutter room with all its fine cabinet and counter space means that the often numerous family projects can be on-going. This room is ideally isolated from the family's daily living patterns. The media room may be thought of as the family's entertainment center. While this is the room for the large or small TV, the home movies, the stereo and VCR equipment, it will serve as the library or study. It would be ideal as the family's home office with its computer equipment. Your family will decide just how it will utilize this outstanding area.

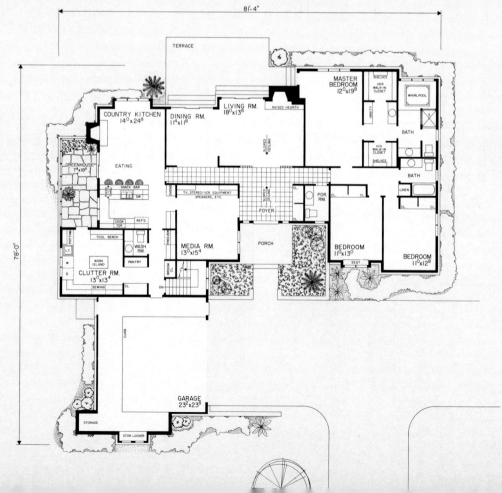

Design 82915 *2,758 Sq. Ft.; 60,850 Cu Ft.*

● The features of this appealing contemporary design go far beyond the clutter and media rooms. The country kitchen is spacious and caters to the family's informal living and dining activities. While it overlooks the rear yard it is just a step from the delightful greenhouse. Many happy hours will be spent here enjoying to the fullest the outdoors from within. The size of the greenhouse is 8'x18' and contains 149 sq. ft. not included in the square foot-

age quoted above. The formal living and dining areas feature spacious open planning. Sloping ceiling in the living room, plus the sliding glass doors to the outdoor terrace enhance the cheerfulness of this area. The foyer is large and routes traffic efficiently to all areas. Guest coat closets and a powder room are handy. The sleeping zone is well-planned. Two children's bedrooms have fine wall space, good wardrobe facilities and a full bath.

The master bedroom is exceptional. It is large enough to accommodate a sitting area and has access to the terrace. Two walk-in closets, a vanity area with lavatory and a compartmented bath are noteworthy features. Observe the stall shower in addition to the dramatic whirlpool installation. The floor plan below is identical with that on the opposite page and shows one of many possible ways to arrange furniture.

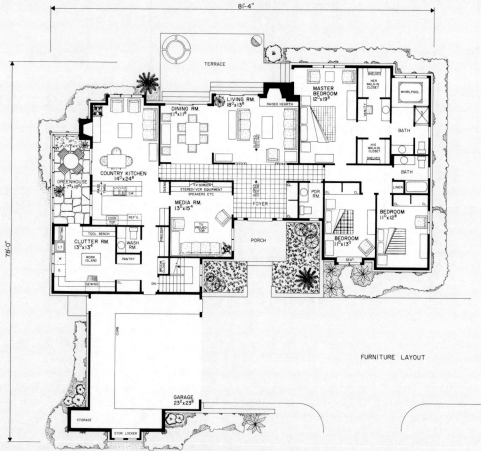

FURNITURE LAYOUT

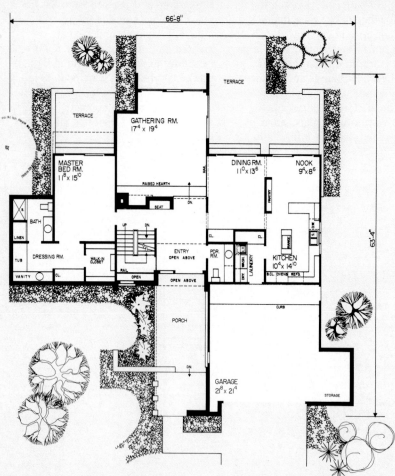

Design 82729

1,590 Sq. Ft. - First Floor
756 Sq. Ft. - Second Floor
39,310 Cu. Ft.

● Entering this home will be a pleasure through the sheltered walk-way to the double front doors. The pleasure and beauty does not stop there. The entry hall and sunken gathering room are open to the upstairs for added dimension. There's even a built-in seat in the entry area. The kitchen-nook area is efficient with its many built-ins and adjacent laundry room. Indoor-outdoor living relationships are excellent. Note the private terrace off the luxurious master bedroom suite, a living terrace accessible from the gathering room, dining room and nook plus the balcony off the upstairs bedroom. Upstairs, there are two bedrooms, each with its own bath and plenty of closets.

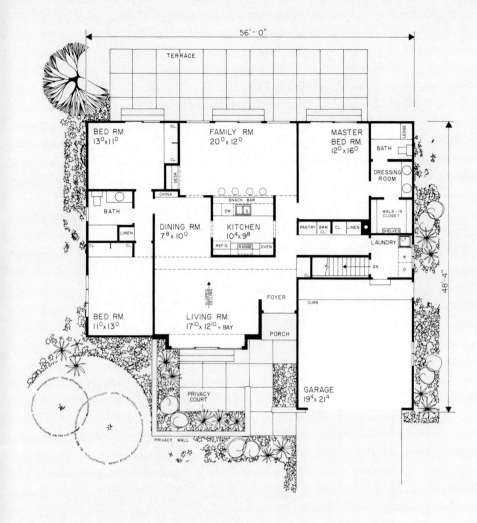

56'-0"

TERRACE

BED RM.
13⁰x11⁰

FAMILY RM.
20⁰x12⁰

MASTER
BED RM.
12⁰x16⁰

BATH

LEDGE

CL

CL

DESK

DRESSING
ROOM

CHINA

BATH

SNACK BAR

DW S

WALK-IN
CLOSET

LINEN

DINING RM.
7⁸x10⁰

KITCHEN
10⁴x9⁸

PANTRY BRM CL LINEN

CL

CL

REF'G RANGE OVEN

SHELVES

LAUNDRY

W

CL

DN

D

SLOPED CEILING

FOYER

CURB

BED RM.
11⁰x13⁰

LIVING RM.
17¹⁰x12¹⁰ + BAY

PORCH

48'-4"

PRIVACY
COURT

GARAGE
19⁴x21⁴

PRIVACY WALL

Design 82796
1,828 Sq. Ft.; 39,990 Cu. Ft.

● One of the many features of this contemporary, one-story design is its front living room. It has a privacy court which shields it from the street. This is a delightful way to be greeted into this home. This plan is termed as "bi-nuclear". This means that the children's and parent's sleeping quarters are separated. In this house, they are at opposite ends of the plan to assure the utmost in privacy. Each area has its own full bath. The interior kitchen is a great idea. It frees up valuable outside wall space for the living area's exclusive use. There is a snack bar in the kitchen/family room for those very informal, quick meals. The dining room is conveniently located near the kitchen. At the garage entrance, the laundry area has plenty of storage closets plus the stairs to the basement. This home will be a welcome addition to any setting.

BEDROOM 11⁰x11⁶ BEDROOM 11⁰x11⁶ WALK-IN CLOSET WALK-IN CLOSET LINEN ROOF BATH DN RAILING CL CL LINEN BEDROOM 12⁴x13⁶ BATH MASTER BEDROOM 13⁰x19²

Design 82808

1,540 Sq. Ft. - First Floor
1,117 Sq. Ft. - Second Floor
605 Sq. Ft. - Apartment
48,075 Cu. Ft.

● A complete apartment is tucked in the back of this Colonial home. This apartment would be ideal for a live-in relative or supplement your income by becoming a landlord and rent out the apartment. Whatever you choose, the occupants will be served by an L-shaped kitchen, living room with bay and dining area, bedroom and bath. A complete unit in itself. The rest of this house will serve a larger family with great ease. There is a formal living room and an informal family room plus a good-sized study. Every family member will have a place to go in this home. Sliding glass doors in the two eating areas, the informal breakfast room and the formal dining room, open to a large terrace. All of the sleeping facilities are on the efficiently planned second floor.

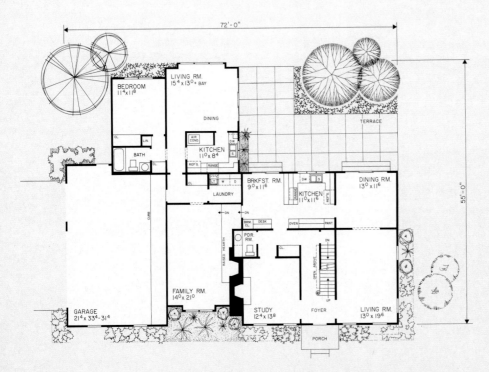

Design 82794

1,680 Sq. Ft. - First Floor
1,165 Sq. Ft. - Second Floor
867 Sq. Ft. - Apartment
55,900 Cu. Ft.

● This exceptionally pleasing Tudor design has a great deal of interior livability to offer its occupants. Use the main entrance, enter into the foyer and begin your journey throughout this design. To the left of the foyer is the study, to the right, the formal living room. The living room leads to the rear, formal dining room. This room has access to the outdoors and is conveniently located adjacent to the kitchen. A snack bar divides the kitchen from the family room which also has access to outdoors plus it has a fireplace as does the living room. The second floor houses the family's four bedrooms. Down six steps from the mud room is the laundry and entrance to the garage, up six steps from this area is a complete apartment. This is an excellent room for a live-in relative. It is completely private by gaining access from the outdoor balcony.

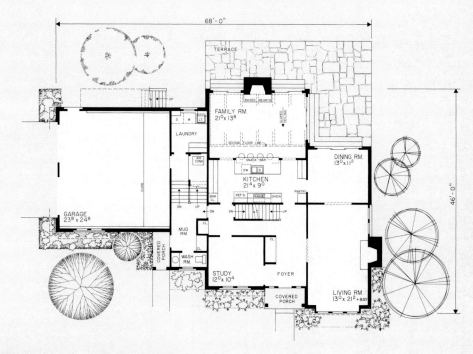

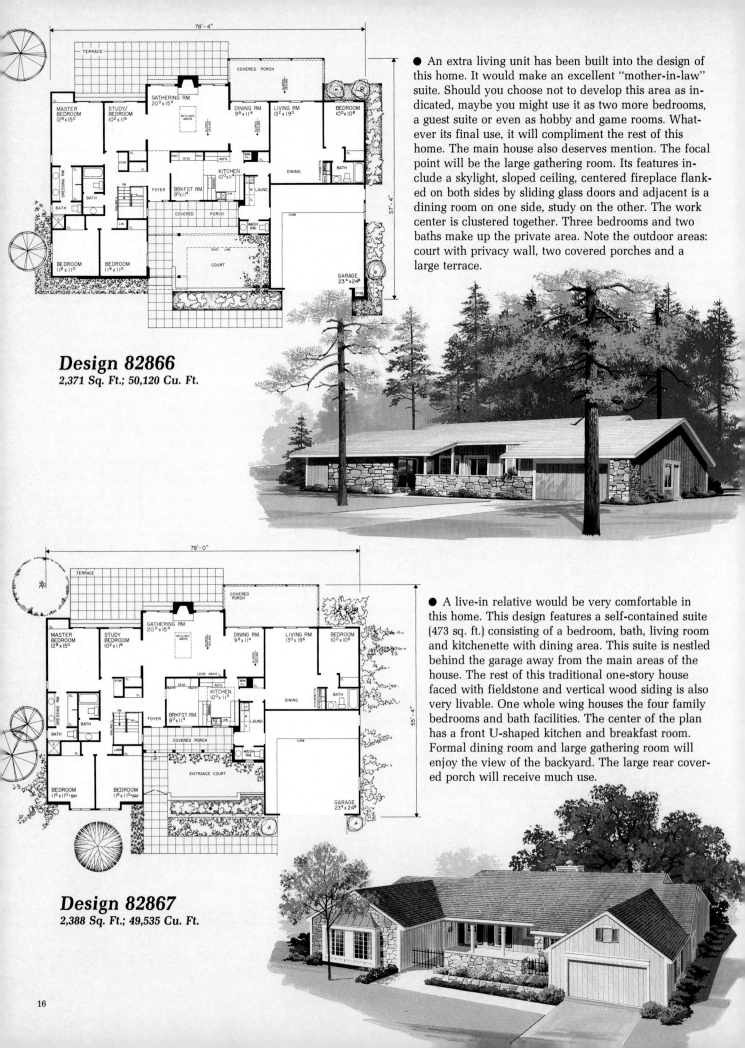

78'-4"

TERRACE

COVERED PORCH

GATHERING RM.
20⁰ x 15⁴

MASTER BEDROOM
12⁸ x 15⁰

STUDY/BEDROOM
10² x 11⁶

DINING RM.
9⁸ x 11⁴

LIVING RM.
13² x 19⁰

BEDROOM
10⁰ x 10⁸

SKYLIGHT ABOVE

DRESSING RM.

STOR

BATH

KITCHEN
10⁰ x 11⁴

FOYER

BRKFST RM.
8⁰ x 11⁴

COVERED PORCH

COURT

DINING

BATH

LAUND.

WASH RM.

CURB

ROOF LINE

BATH

BEDROOM
11⁶ x 11⁰

BEDROOM
11⁶ x 11⁰

GARAGE
23⁴ x 24⁸

57'-4"

Design 82866
2,371 Sq. Ft.; 50,120 Cu. Ft.

● An extra living unit has been built into the design of this home. It would make an excellent "mother-in-law" suite. Should you choose not to develop this area as indicated, maybe you might use it as two more bedrooms, a guest suite or even as hobby and game rooms. Whatever its final use, it will compliment the rest of this home. The main house also deserves mention. The focal point will be the large gathering room. Its features include a skylight, sloped ceiling, centered fireplace flanked on both sides by sliding glass doors and adjacent is a dining room on one side, study on the other. The work center is clustered together. Three bedrooms and two baths make up the private area. Note the outdoor areas: court with privacy wall, two covered porches and a large terrace.

78'-0"

TERRACE

COVERED PORCH

GATHERING RM.
20⁰ x 15⁴

MASTER BEDROOM
12⁸ x 15⁰

STUDY/BEDROOM
10² x 11⁶

DINING RM.
9⁸ x 11⁴

LIVING RM.
13⁰ x 19⁶

BEDROOM
10⁰ x 10⁸

SKYLIGHT ABOVE

LEDGE ABOVE

DRESSING RM.

STOR

BATH

KITCHEN
10⁰ x 11⁴

FOYER

BRKFST RM.
8⁰ x 11⁴

COVERED PORCH

ENTRANCE COURT

DINING

BATH

LAUND.

WASH RM.

CURB

BATH

BEDROOM
11⁶ x 11⁰ BAY

BEDROOM
11⁶ x 11⁰ BAY

GARAGE
23⁴ x 24⁸

55'-4"

Design 82867
2,388 Sq. Ft.; 49,535 Cu. Ft.

● A live-in relative would be very comfortable in this home. This design features a self-contained suite (473 sq. ft.) consisting of a bedroom, bath, living room and kitchenette with dining area. This suite is nestled behind the garage away from the main areas of the house. The rest of this traditional one-story house faced with fieldstone and vertical wood siding is also very livable. One whole wing houses the four family bedrooms and bath facilities. The center of the plan has a front U-shaped kitchen and breakfast room. Formal dining room and large gathering room will enjoy the view of the backyard. The large rear covered porch will receive much use.

Heritage Houses
Recapturing the Charm of Early America

Design 82132 *1,958 Sq. Ft. - First Floor; 1,305 Sq. Ft. - Second Floor 51,428 Cu. Ft.*

● This Georgian adaptation gets its appeal from its quietly formal facade. The identifying characteristics of this exterior include the symmetry of the window arrangement, the detailing of the doorway, the massive end chimneys, the tight cornices, the delicate dentils and the raised level of the entrance. The development of the rear yard to include formal gardens is consistent with the atmosphere created by the design of the house itself. Access to the garden area may be gained through the service door, the family room and the garage. This floor plan deserves a full measure of careful study. It will be an enjoyable exercise to visualize how you and your family will live in this home. Each room seems to have its own set of features. The living room, for instance, has as its focal point a corner fireplace and plenty of privacy. An abundance of floor space and two china storage niches are in the dining room. The kitchen area has a beamed ceiling and a big breakfast area. A second fireplace is in the family room. Upstairs, there is a fine master bedroom and two family bedrooms.

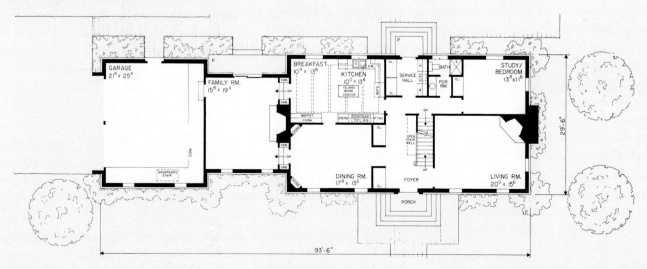

Design 81887

1,518 Sq. Ft. - First Floor
1,144 Sq. Ft. - Second Floor
40,108 Cu. Ft.

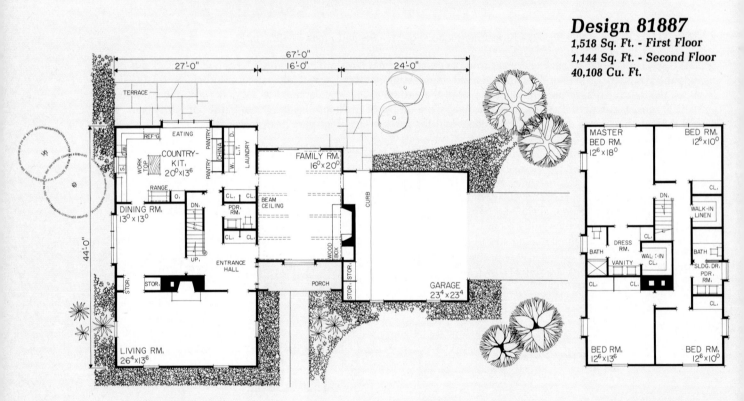

● This Gambrel roof Colonial is steeped in history. Various roof planes, window treatment and a rambling nature of the entire house revives a picture of rural New England. All of its pleasing proportions are a delight to the eye. The covered porch protects the front door which opens into a spacious entrance hall. Traffic then flows in an orderly fashion to the end living room, the separate dining room, the cozy family room and the country kitchen. The country kitchen is spacious and efficiently planned. Other first floor features include a laundry room, plenty of coat closets and a handy powder room. Two fireplaces enliven the decor of the living areas. Upstairs, there is an exceptional master bedroom suite. Note walk-in closet in the bath area. The three children's bedrooms are serviced by a compartmented main bath. This design will adapt readily to either an interior or corner lot.

Design 82320 *1,856 Sq. Ft. - First Floor; 1,171 Sq. Ft. - Second Floor; 46,699 Cu. Ft.*

● A charming Colonial adaptation with a Gambrel roof front exterior and a Salt Box rear. The focal point of family activities will be the spacious family kitchen with its beamed ceiling and fireplace. Blueprints include details for both three and four bedroom options. In addition to the family kitchen, note the family room with beamed ceiling and fireplace. Don't miss the study with built-in book shelves and cabinets. Gracious living will be enjoyed throughout this design.

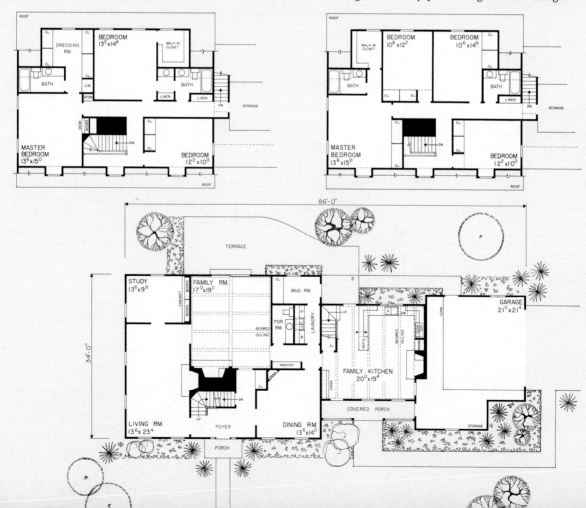

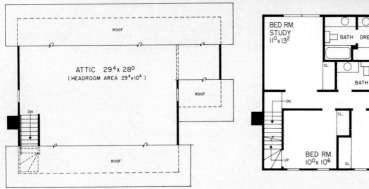

ATTIC 29⁴ x 28⁰
(HEADROOM AREA 29⁴ x 10⁶)

ROOF

ROOF

ROOF

DN

BED RM.
STUDY
11⁰ x 13²

BATH

DRESSING RM.

VANITY

MASTER
BED RM.
13⁰ x 13²

CL.

CL.

BATH

CL.

CL.

DN.

CL.

LIN.

CL.

CL.

UP

BED RM.
10⁰ x 10⁶

CL.

BED RM.
13⁰ x 10⁶

Design 82774
1,370 Sq. Ft. - First Floor
969 Sq. Ft. - Second Floor
38,305 Cu. Ft.

● A Farmhouse adaptation with all of the most up-to-date features expected in a new home. Beginning with the formal areas, this design offers pleasures for the entire family. There is the quiet, corner living room which has an opening to the sizable dining room. This room will have plenty of natural light from the delightful bay window which overlooks the rear yard. It is also conveniently located with the efficient, U-shaped kitchen just a step away. The kitchen features many built-ins with a pass-thru to the beamed ceiling breakfast room. Sliding glass doors to the terrace are fine attractions in both the sunken family room and breakfast room. The service entrance to the garage has a storage closet on each side, plus there is a secondary entrance through the laundry area. Recreational activities and hobbies can be pursued in the basement area. Four bedrooms and two baths are on the second floor.

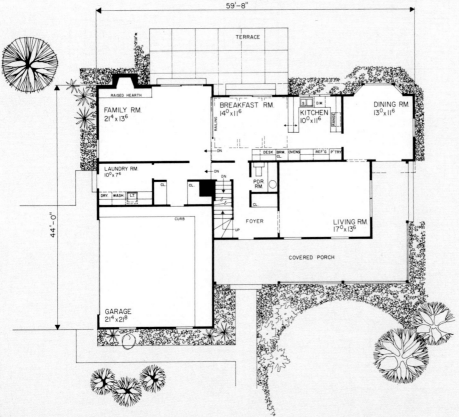

59'-8"

TERRACE

RAISED HEARTH

FAMILY RM.
21⁴ x 13⁶

BREAKFAST RM.
14⁰ x 11⁶

KITCHEN
10⁰ x 11⁶

DINING RM.
13⁰ x 11⁶

RAILING

S

D.W.

RANGE

LAUNDRY RM.
10⁰ x 7⁶

DN

DESK

BRM.

OVENS

CL.

REF'G

P'TRY

DRY.

WASH.

CL.

CL.

DN

PDR
RM.

LIVING RM.
17⁰ x 13⁶

CURB

DN

UP

FOYER

44'-0"

GARAGE
21⁴ x 21⁸

COVERED PORCH

BEDROOM 11⁰ x 12⁴

BEDROOM 12⁰ x 10⁰

WALK-IN CLOSET

BATH

DRESSING RM.

LINEN

BEDROOM 16⁰ x 12⁴

BATH

MASTER BEDROOM 16⁰ x 13⁶

COVERED BALCONY

Design 82664

1,308 Sq. Ft. - First Floor
1,262 Sq. Ft. - Second Floor
49,215 Cu. Ft.

● The exterior of this full two-story is highlighted by the covered, front porch and the covered, second floor balcony. Many enjoyable hours will be spent at these outdoor areas. There is also a rear terrace. It is accessible by way of the two dining areas. The interior is highlighted by a spacious country kitchen. Be sure to notice its island cook-top, fireplace and the beamed ceiling. It is also conveniently located. The laundry, rear terrace, basement stairs and dining room are only steps away. The front of this plan is devoted to the two living areas. To the left of the foyer is the formal living room, to the right, the family room. A built-in bar is in the family room. Sleeping facilities are on the second floor. All four bedrooms are a good size. The spacious master bath is outstanding. Study the many other fine details of this home.

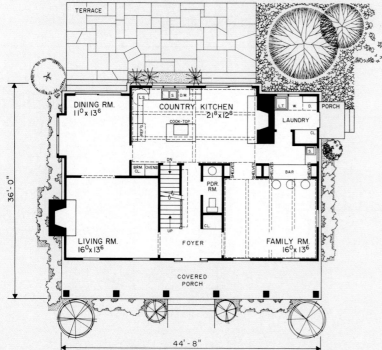

TERRACE

DINING RM. 11⁰ x 13⁶

COUNTRY KITCHEN 21⁸ x 12⁸

COOK-TOP

LAUNDRY

PORCH

BRM. CL.

OVENS

DN

PDR. RM.

BAR

36' 0"

LIVING RM. 16⁰ x 13⁶

UP

FOYER

FAMILY RM. 16⁰ x 13⁶

COVERED PORCH

44' - 8"

Design 82661 1,020 Sq. Ft. - First Floor
777 Sq. Ft. - Second Floor; 30,745 Cu. Ft.

● This compact starter house or retirement home houses a very livable plan. An outstanding feature is the large country kitchen. Its fine attractions include a beamed ceiling, raised hearth fireplace, built-in window seat and a door leading to the outdoors. A living room is in the front of the plan and has another fireplace. The second floor houses the sleeping and bath facilities.

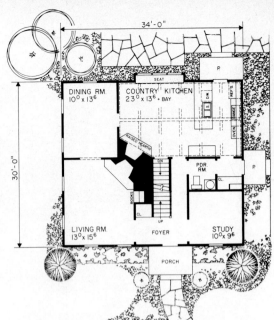

Design 82655 893 Sq. Ft. - First Floor
652 Sq. Ft. - Second Floor; 22,555 Cu. Ft.

● Wonderful things can be enclosed in small packages. This one-and-a-half story design is one of those cases. The total area is a mere 1,545 square feet yet its features are many, indeed. Its exterior appeal is very eye-pleasing with horizontal lines and two second story dormers. Livability will be enjoyed in this plan. The study is ideal for a quiet escape. A powder room is convenient to the kitchen and breakfast room. Two bedrooms and two baths are on the second floor.

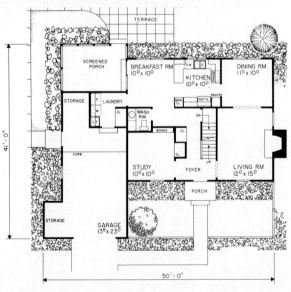

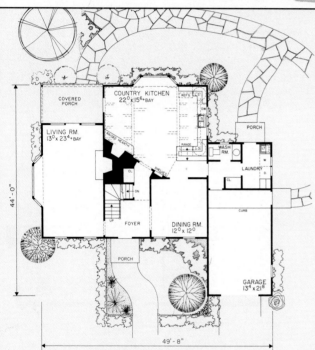

Design 82657

1,217 Sq. Ft. - First Floor
868 Sq. Ft. - Second Floor
33,260 Cu. Ft.

● Deriving its design from the traditional Cape Cod style, this facade features clapboard siding, small-paned windows and a transom-lit entrance flanked by carriage lamps. A central chimney services two fireplaces, one in the country-kitchen and the other in the formal living room. The master suite is to the left of the upstairs landing. A full bathroom services two additional bedrooms.

Design 82192 1,884 Sq. Ft. - First Floor
1,521 Sq. Ft. - Second Floor; 58,380 Cu. Ft.

● This is surely a fine adaptation from the 18th-Century when for-
mality and elegance were by-words. The authentic detailing of this
design centers around the fine proportions, the dentils, the window
symmetry, the front door and entranceway, the massive chimneys and
the masonry work. The rear elevation retains all the grandeur exem-
plary of exquisite architecture. The appeal of this outstanding home
does not end with its exterior elevations. Consider the formal living
room with its corner fireplace. Also, the library with its wall of
bookshelves and cabinets. Further, the dining room highlights corner
china cabinets. Continue to study this elegant plan.

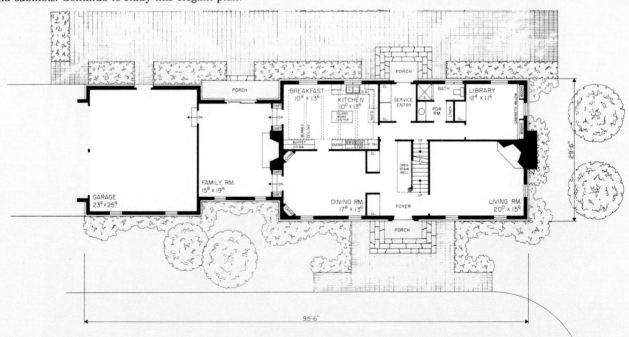

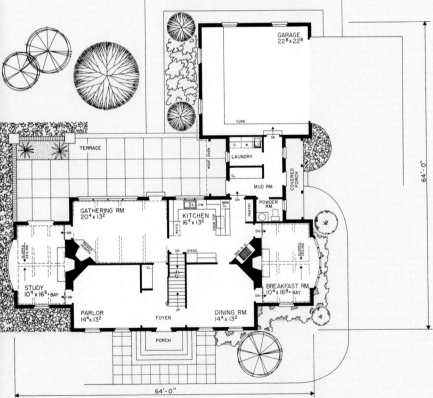

Design 82662

**1,735 Sq. Ft. - First Floor; 1,075 Sq. Ft. - Second Floor
746 Sq. Ft. - Third Floor; 49,165 Cu. Ft.**

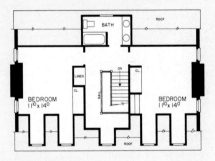

● Influences from both Georgian and Federal architecture are apparent in the design of this home. The exterior is highlighted with multi-paned windows, two classic chimneys and well-proportioned dormers. A curved window is visible in each wing. The interior of this design has been planned just as carefully as the exterior. Study each area carefully and imagine how your family would utilize the space. There is a study, parlor, gathering room, U-shaped kitchen, formal and informal dining rooms plus a powder room and laundry. That is a lot of livability on one floor. Plus - three fireplaces! Three bedrooms and two baths are on the second floor. Two more bedrooms and another bath are on the third floor. A lack of space will never be a problem in this house.

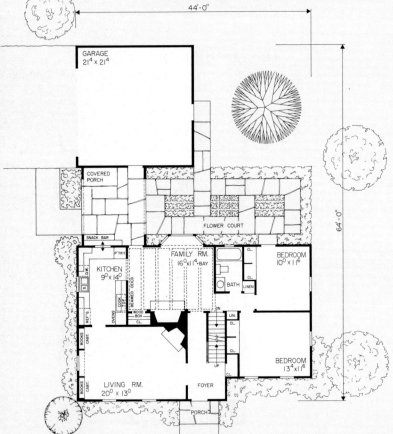

Design 82145 1,182 Sq. Ft. - First Floor
708 Sq. Ft. - Second Floor; 28,303 Cu. Ft.

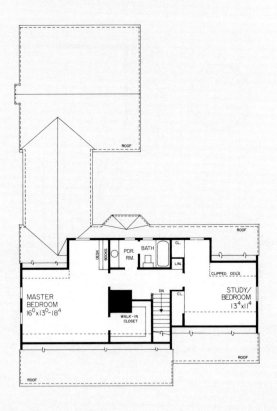

● This authentic adaptation, historically referred to as a "half house", has its roots in the heritage of New England. One of the many features of this house is that it can be developed in stages. Seeing that there are two bedrooms and a full bath on the first floor, the second floor can be developed at a later date for an additional two bedrooms and another full bath. This would double your sleeping capacity. Notice that the overall width of this design is only 44 feet. And, because of its configuration, it is ideal for a corner lot. Observe the covered porch which leads to the garage and the flower court. An in-line version of this plan is Design 82146. It, of course, requires a wider and more spacious piece of property. And, it too, has two fireplaces, one in each of the living areas.

BEDROOM 12⁰x13⁶
BEDROOM 13⁰x10⁰
BATH
PDR. RM.
ROOF
CL
CL
CL
DN
LINEN
BRM CL
BEDROOM 14⁰x13⁰
ATTIC ACCESS
CL
DRESSING RM.
BATH
MASTER BEDROOM 18⁸x13⁶
WALK-IN CLOSET
ROOF
S

Design 82211

1,214 Sq. Ft. - First Floor
1,146 Sq. Ft. - Second Floor
32,752 Cu. Ft.

● The appeal of this Colonial home will be virtually everlasting. It will improve with age and service the growing family well. Imagine your family living here. There are four bedrooms, 2½ baths, plus plenty of first floor living space. Formal and informal activities will have their place. Entertaining can be done in the front living room. It is spacious and has an end fireplace. When dinner is ready, your guests can flow to the adjacent dining room. Maybe an after dinner drink could be served on the terrace. There are sliding glass doors in the dining room which lead to this outdoor area. There is a second set of doors to the terrace in the family room. This will be a warm and comfortable area for family and friends alike. The adjacent work center is efficient. Note the powder room which is convenient to all of the first floor areas.

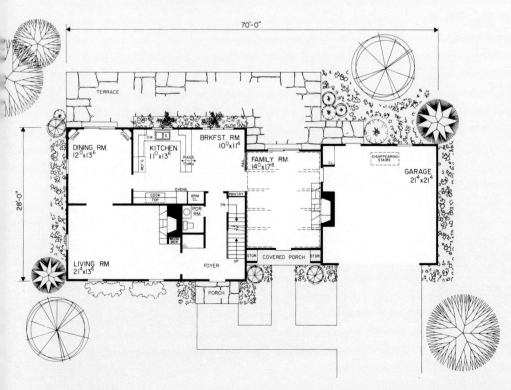

70'-0"

28'-0"

TERRACE
DINING RM. 12⁰x13⁶
KITCHEN 11⁰x13⁶
D.W. S
BRKFST. RM. 10⁰x11⁴
PASS THRU
FAMILY RM. 14⁰x17⁸
RAIL
DISAPPEARING STAIRS
GARAGE 21⁴x21⁴
CL
REF'G.
COOK TOP
OVENS
BRM CL
PANTRY
DN
PDR. RM.
WOOD BOX
CL
FOYER
UP
STOR.
COVERED PORCH
STOR.
LIVING RM. 21⁴x13⁶
PORCH

Design 82230 2,288 Sq. Ft. - First Floor
1,863 Sq. Ft. - Second Floor; 79,736 Cu. Ft.

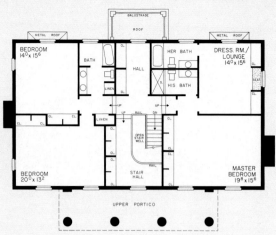

● The gracefulness and appeal of this southern adaptation will be everlasting. The imposing, two-story portico is truly dramatic. Notice the authentic detailing of the tapered Doric columns, balustraded roof deck, denticulated cornice, front entrance and shuttered windows. The architecture of the rear is no less appealing with its formal symmetry and smaller Doric portico. The spacious, formal entrance hall provides a fitting introduction to the scale and elegance of the interior. Observe the openness of the stairwell which provides a view of the curving balusters above. The large living room with its colonial fireplace enjoys a full measure of privacy. Across the hall is the formal dining room with built-in china cabinets. Beamed ceilings and plenty of space produce a country style kitchen. The island work center will be just one of your favorite convenience features. A compartmented full bath is handy to the service entrance and the isolated library, which may double as a guest room when the occasion demands. Functioning between the house and the garage is the sunken family room. It stretches the full width of the house. Two family bedrooms are on the second floor with the master bedroom suite. Imagine yourself occupying this outstanding area. "His" and "her" baths, lounge/dressing room and an abundance of closet space highlight this area.

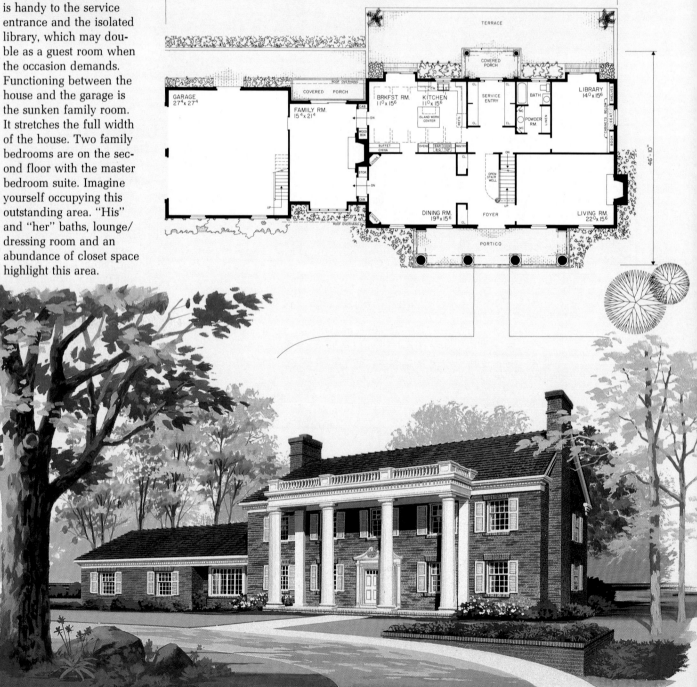

Design 82283

1,559 Sq. Ft. - First Floor
1,404 Sq. Ft. - Second Floor
48,606 Cu. Ft.

● Reminiscent of the stately character of Federal architecture during an earlier period in our history, this two-story is replete with exquisite detailing. The cornice work, the pediment gable, the dentils, the brick quions at the corners, the beautifully proportioned columns, the front door detailing, the window treatment and massive twin chimneys are among the features which make this design so unique. The formal, center entrance hall controls traffic to all areas. To the left are the formal areas, the living and dining rooms. To the right are the informal family and quiet study rooms. Straight ahead is the kitchen with its informal eating space. Upstairs, there are four bedrooms and two baths with an abundance of storage space. Be sure to notice such other features as the two fireplaces, the mud room, the wash room, the powder room, the beamed ceiling, etc.

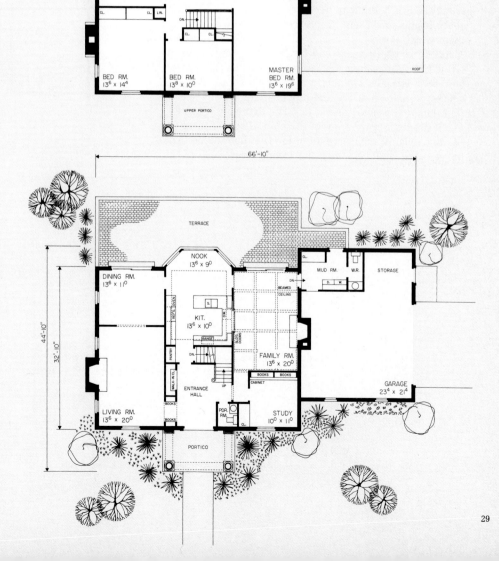

Design 82596 1,489 Sq. Ft. - First Floor
982 Sq. Ft. - Second Floor; 38,800 Cu. Ft.

● Captivating as a New England village! From the weather-vane atop the garage to the covered side entry and paned windows, this home is perfectly detailed. It has lots of living space inside, too. There is an exceptionally large family room which is more than 29' x 13', including the dining area. A raised hearth fireplace and double doors leading to the terrace are in this area. The adjoining kitchen features an island cook-top plus cabinets, a built-in oven and lots of counter space. Attractive and efficient! Steps away is a first floor laundry. Formal rooms, too! The living and dining rooms are both in the front of the plan. Between them is a powder room. It will serve all of the first floor areas. All of the sleeping facilities are on the second floor.

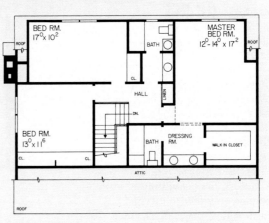

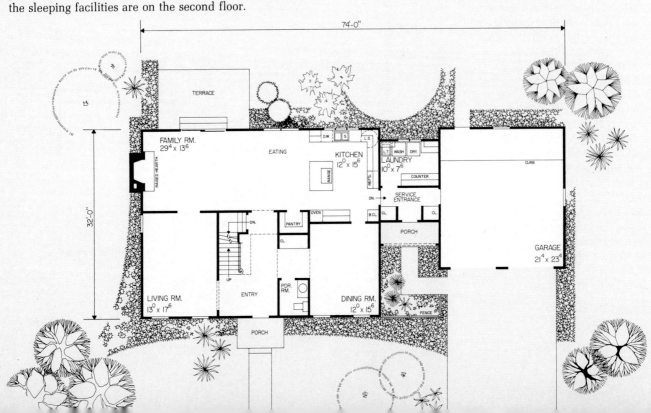

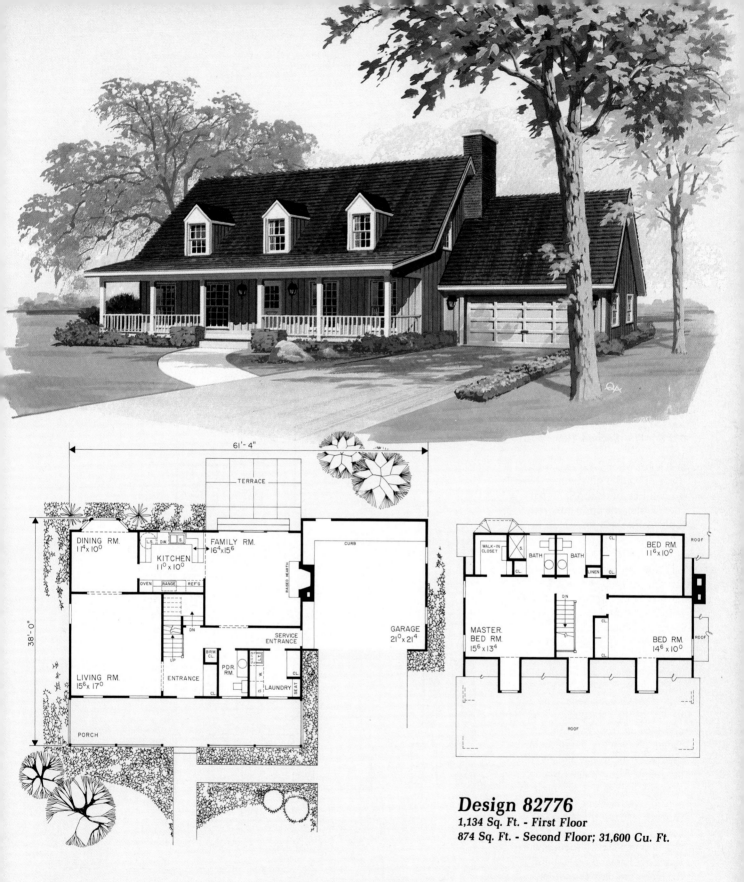

TERRACE

DINING RM. 11⁴ x 10⁰

KITCHEN 11⁰ x 10⁰

OVEN RANGE REF'G

FAMILY RM. 16⁴ x 15⁶

CURB

GARAGE 21⁰ x 21⁴

RAISED HEARTH

SERVICE ENTRANCE

LIVING RM. 15⁶ x 17⁰

UP DN

B.RM. CL.

PDR. RM.

W. D.

LAUNDRY

SEAT

CL.

ENTRANCE

CL.

PORCH

61'-4"

38'-0"

WALK-IN CLOSET

S.

BATH

BATH

CL.

LINEN

CL.

CL.

BED RM. 11⁶ x 10⁰

ROOF

MASTER. BED RM. 15⁶ x 13⁴

DN

CL.

CL.

BED RM. 14⁶ x 10⁰

ROOF

ROOF

Design 82776
1,134 Sq. Ft. - First Floor
874 Sq. Ft. - Second Floor; 31,600 Cu. Ft.

● This board-and-batten farmhouse design has all of the country charm of New England. The large front covered porch surely will be appreciated during the beautiful warm weather months. Immediately off the front entrance is the delightful corner living room. The dining room with bay window will be easily served by the U-shaped kitchen. Informal family living enjoyment will be obtained in the family room which features a raised hearth fireplace, sliding glass doors to the rear terrace and easy access to the work center of powder room, laundry and service entrance. The second floor houses all of the sleeping facilities. There is a master bedroom with a private bath and walk-in closet. Two other bedrooms share a bath. This is an excellent one-and-a-half story design.

Design 82615 2,563 Sq. Ft. - First Floor
552 Sq. Ft. - Second Floor; 59,513 Cu. Ft.

● The exterior detailing of this design recalls 18th-Century New England architecture. The narrow clapboards and shuttered, multi-paned windows help its detail. Arched entryways forming covered porches lead to the master bedroom and the other to the service entrance. Enter by way of the centered front door and you are greeted into the foyer. Directly to the right is the study or optional bedroom or to the left is the living room. This large formal room features a fireplace and sliding glass doors to the sun-drenched solarium. The beauty of the solarium will be appreciated from two other rooms besides the living room; the master bedroom and the dining room. All of these rooms have sliding glass doors for easy access. The work center will function efficiently. When it comes time for informal living, this design's family room is outstanding. Beamed ceiling and fireplace are only two of its many features. In addition to the first floor master bedroom, there are two bedrooms and a bath upstairs. The detailing that this design offers will be appreciated for a lifetime by every member of the family.

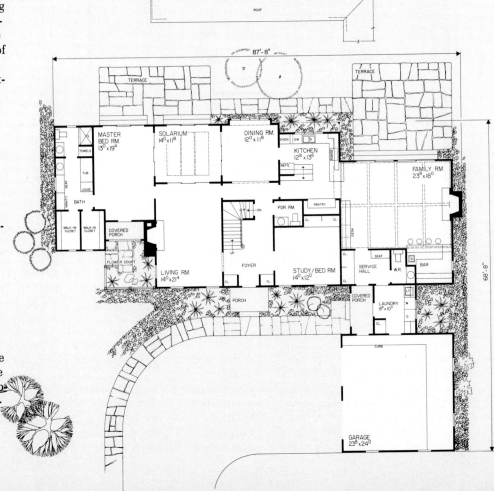

Energy-Oriented Designs
Fostering the Benefits of Solar Planning

Design 82830 *1,795 Sq. Ft. - Main Level; 1,546 Sq. Ft. - Lower Level; 49,900 Cu. Ft.*

● Outstanding contemporary design! This home has been created with the advantages of passive solar heating in mind. For optimum energy savings, this delightful design combines passive solar devices, the solarium, with optional active, collectors. Included with the purchase of this design are four plot plans to assure that the solar collectors will face the south. The garage in each plan acts as a buffer against cold northern winds. Schematic details for solar application also are included. Along with being energy-efficient, this design has excellent living patterns. Three bedrooms, the master bedroom on the main level and two others on the lower level at each side of the solarium. The living area of the main level will be able to enjoy the delightful view of the solarium and sunken garden.

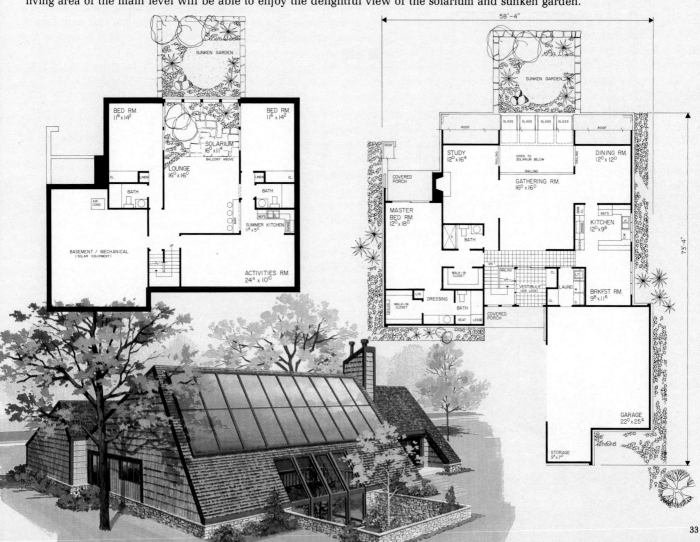

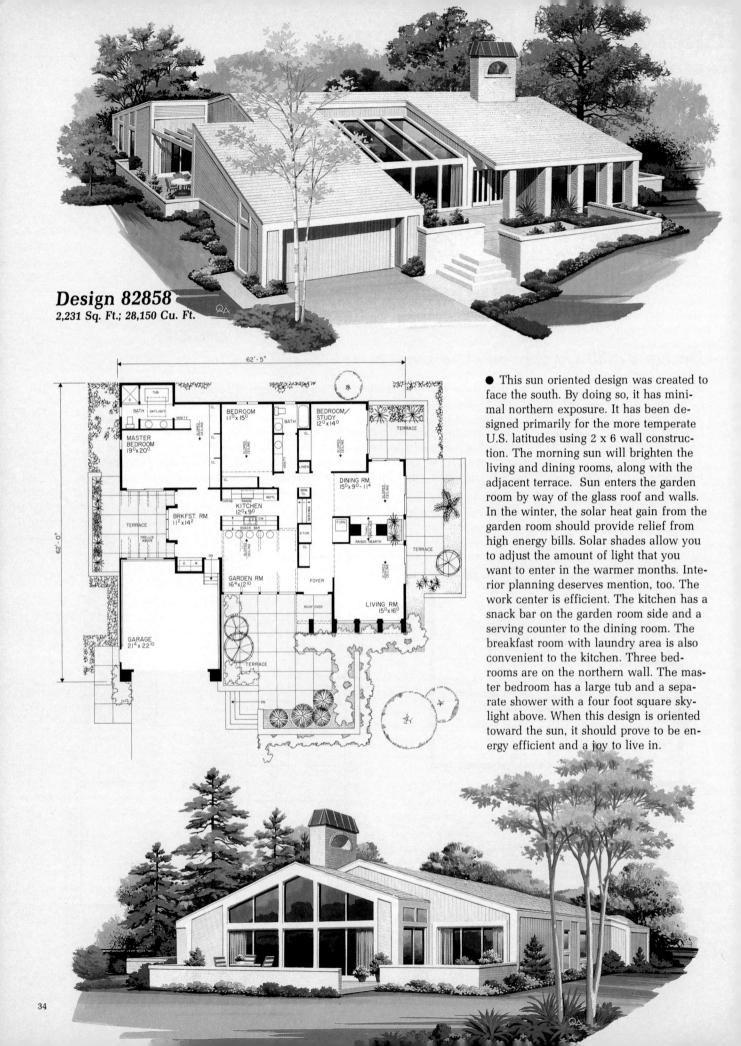

Design 82858
2,231 Sq. Ft.; 28,150 Cu. Ft.

● This sun oriented design was created to face the south. By doing so, it has minimal northern exposure. It has been designed primarily for the more temperate U.S. latitudes using 2 x 6 wall construction. The morning sun will brighten the living and dining rooms, along with the adjacent terrace. Sun enters the garden room by way of the glass roof and walls. In the winter, the solar heat gain from the garden room should provide relief from high energy bills. Solar shades allow you to adjust the amount of light that you want to enter in the warmer months. Interior planning deserves mention, too. The work center is efficient. The kitchen has a snack bar on the garden room side and a serving counter to the dining room. The breakfast room with laundry area is also convenient to the kitchen. Three bedrooms are on the northern wall. The master bedroom has a large tub and a separate shower with a four foot square skylight above. When this design is oriented toward the sun, it should prove to be energy efficient and a joy to live in.

Design 82827 1,618 Sq. Ft. - Upper Level
1,458 Sq. Ft. - Lower Level; 41,370 Cu. Ft.

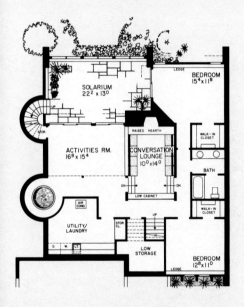

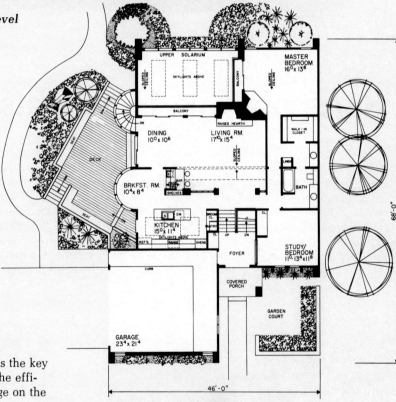

● The two-story solarium with skylights above is the key to energy savings to this bi-level design. Study the efficiency of this floor plan. The conversation lounge on the lower level is a unique focal point.

A Sunspace Spa Highlights this Trend House

● Contemporary in exterior styling, this house is energy oriented. It calls for 2x6 exterior wall construction with placement on a north facing lot. Traffic flows through the interior of this plan by way of the foyer. Not only is the foyer useful, but it is dramatic with its sloped ceiling and second floor balcony and skylight above. Excellent living areas are throughout. A spacious, sunken living room is to the left of the foyer. It shares a thru-fireplace, faced with fieldstone, with the study. Sloped ceilings are in both of these rooms. Informal activities can take place in the family room. It, too, has a fireplace and is adjacent to the work center. Two of the bedrooms are on the second floor with a lounge overlooking the gathering room below. The master bedroom is on the first floor. A generous amount of closet space with mirrored doors will enhance its appearance. Study the spacious master bath. It has direct access to the sunspace spa.

Design 82900 *2,332 Sq. Ft. - First Floor; 953 Sq. Ft. - Second Floor; 46,677 Cu. Ft.*

Passive solar benefits will be acquired from the spa. It transmits light and heat to the other parts of the house. Heat stored during the day, by the stone floor, will be circulated at night by mechanical means. Shades may be used to control the amount of heat gain into this area. This spa provides a large area where various activities can be done at the same time. Note the bar, whirlpool and exercise area. It will be a cheerful and spacious family recreation area. There are 551 square feet and 9,200 cubic feet in the sunspace spa which are not included in the above totals.

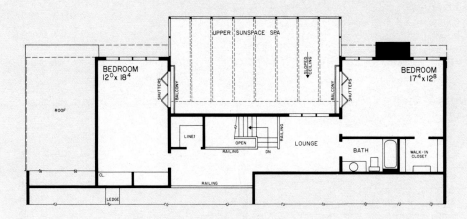

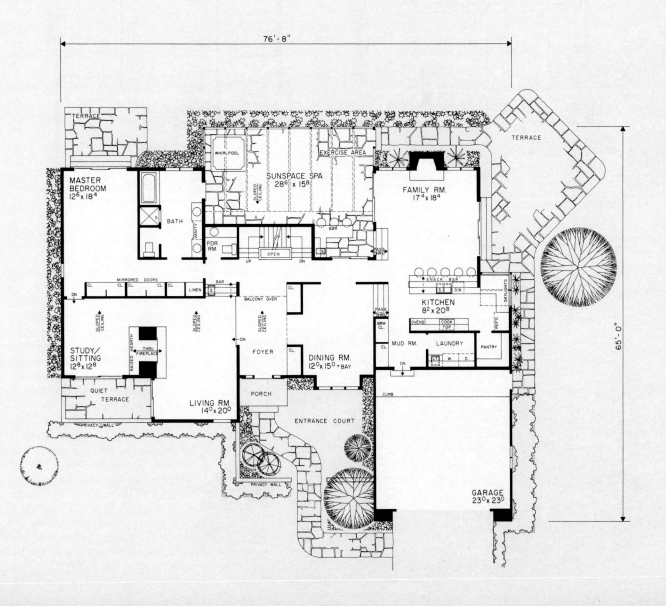

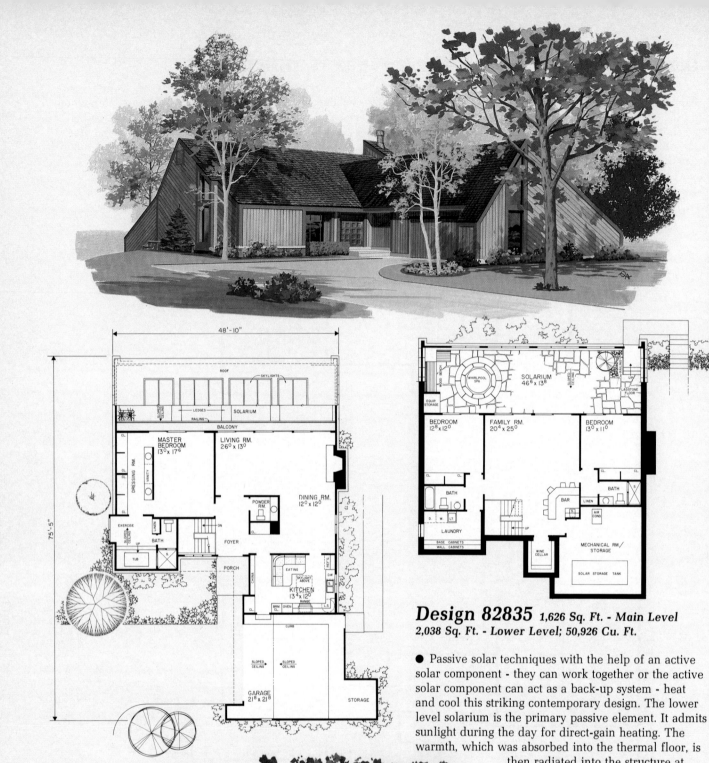

48'-10"

75'-5"

ROOF

SKYLIGHTS

LEDGES   SOLARIUM

RAILING

BALCONY

MASTER BEDROOM 13⁰ x 17⁶

LIVING RM. 26⁰ x 13⁰

DRESSING RM.

VANITY

CL

CL

POWDER RM.

DINING RM. 12⁰ x 12⁰

EXERCISE

LINEN

BATH

TUB

UP

FOYER

DN

PORCH

CHINA

EATING

SKYLIGHT ABOVE

KITCHEN 13⁴ x 12⁰

BRM. OVEN   RANGE

REF.

L.S.

SLOPED CEILING   SLOPED CEILING

CURB

GARAGE 21⁸ x 21⁸

STORAGE

SOLARIUM 46⁶ x 13⁸

WHIRLPOOL SPA

EQUIP STORAGE

FLAGSTONE FLOOR

UP

BEDROOM 12⁸ x 12⁰

FAMILY RM. 20⁴ x 25⁰

BEDROOM 13⁰ x 11⁰

CL   CL

CL   CL

BATH

BAR   LINEN

BATH

D. W. LT

AIR COND

LAUNDRY

UP

BASE CABINETS
WALL CABINETS

WINE CELLAR

MECHANICAL RM./ STORAGE

SOLAR STORAGE TANK

Design 82835 *1,626 Sq. Ft. - Main Level*
2,038 Sq. Ft. - Lower Level; 50,926 Cu. Ft.

● Passive solar techniques with the help of an active solar component - they can work together or the active solar component can act as a back-up system - heat and cool this striking contemporary design. The lower level solarium is the primary passive element. It admits sunlight during the day for direct-gain heating. The warmth, which was absorbed into the thermal floor, is then radiated into the structure at night. The earth berms on the three sides of the lower level help keep out the winter cold and summer heat. The active system uses collector panels to gather the sun's heat. The heat is transferred via a water pipe system to the lower level storage tank where it is circulated throughout the house by a heat exchanger. Note that where active solar collectors are a design OPTION, which they are in all of our active/passive designs, they must be contracted locally. The collector area must be tailored to the climate and sun angles that characterize your building location.

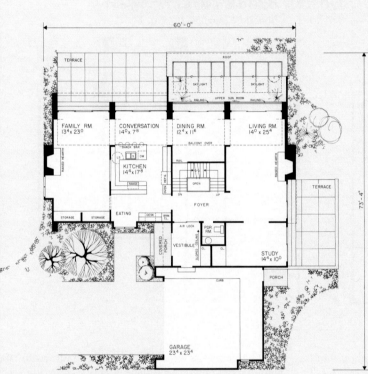

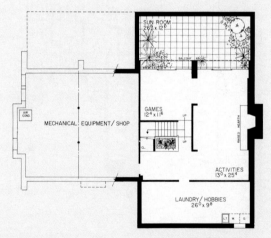

Design 82834

1,775 Sq. Ft. - Main Level; 1,041 Sq. Ft. - Upper Level
1,128 Sq. Ft. - Lower Level; 55,690 Cu. Ft.

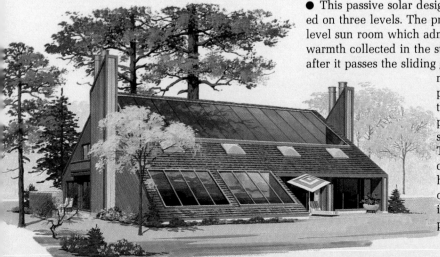

● This passive solar design offers 4,200 square feet of livability situated on three levels. The primary passive element will be the lower level sun room which admits sunlight for direct-gain heating. The solar warmth collected in the sun room will radiate into the rest of the house after it passes the sliding glass doors. During the warm summer months, shades are put over the skylight to protect it from direct sunlight. This design has the option of incorporating active solar heating panels to the roof. The collectors would be installed on the south-facing portion of the roof. They would absorb the sun's warmth for both domestic water and supplementary space heating. An attic fan exhausts any hot air out of the house in the summer and circulates air in the winter. With or without the active solar panels, this is a marvelous contemporary.

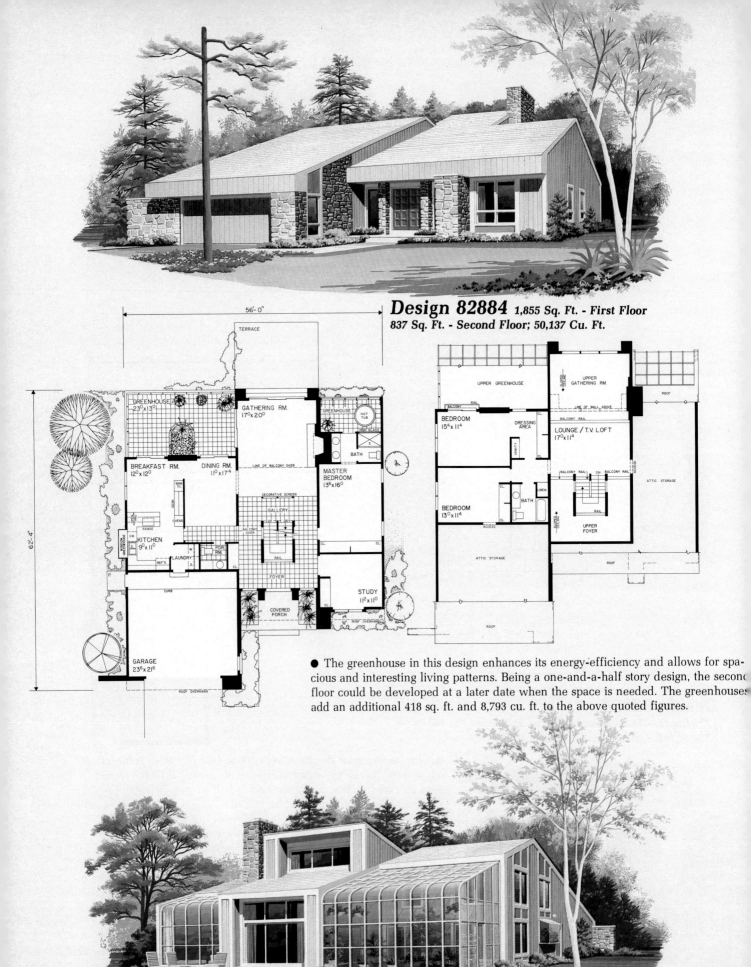

Design 82884   1,855 Sq. Ft. - First Floor
837 Sq. Ft. - Second Floor; 50,137 Cu. Ft.

56'-0"

62'-4"

TERRACE

GREENHOUSE
23⁰x13⁰

GATHERING RM.
17⁰x20⁰

GREENHOUSE

HOT TUB

HIGH GLASS

BATH

BREAKFAST RM.
12⁰x12⁰

DINING RM.
11⁰x17⁴

LINE OF BALCONY OVER

MASTER BEDROOM
13⁶x16⁰

BRM. CL.

DECORATIVE SCREEN

GALLERY

DESK

OVENS

BALCONY OVER

RANGE

KITCHEN
9⁰x11⁰

WINDOW GREENHOUSE

DW.

PDR. RM.

CL.

LAUNDRY

W D

REF'G.

RAIL

FOYER

CL.

STUDY
11²x11⁰

CURB

COVERED PORCH

ROOF OVERHANG

ROOF OVERHANG

GARAGE
23⁶x21⁶

UPPER GREENHOUSE

UPPER GATHERING RM.

ROOF

BALCONY

RAIL

BEDROOM
15⁴x11⁴

DRESSING AREA

VANITY

BALCONY RAIL

LOUNGE / T.V. LOFT
17⁰x11⁴

CL.

BEDROOM
13⁰x11⁴

CL.

BATH

LINEN

BALCONY RAIL

DN BALCONY RAIL

RAIL

ATTIC STORAGE

ACCESS

UPPER FOYER

ACCESS

ATTIC STORAGE

ROOF

ROOF

● The greenhouse in this design enhances its energy-efficiency and allows for spacious and interesting living patterns. Being a one-and-a-half story design, the second floor could be developed at a later date when the space is needed. The greenhouses add an additional 418 sq. ft. and 8,793 cu. ft. to the above quoted figures.

Design 82886
1,733 Sq. Ft.; 34,986 Cu. Ft.

● This one-story house is attractive with its contemporary exterior. It has many excellent features to keep you and your family happy for many years. For example, notice the spacious gathering room with sliding glass doors that allow easy access to the greenhouse. Another exciting feature of this room is that you will receive an abundance of sunshine through the clerestory windows. Also, this plan offers you two nice-sized bedrooms. The master suite is not only roomy but also unique because through both the bedroom and the bath you can enter a greenhouse with a hot tub. The hot tub will be greatly appreciated after a long, hard day at work. Don't forget to note the breakfast room with access to the terrace. You will enjoy the efficient kitchen that will make preparing meals a breeze. A greenhouse window here is charming. An appealing, open staircase leads to the basement. The square and cubic footages of the greenhouses are 394 and 4,070 respectively and are not included in the above figures.

Design 82832

2,805 Sq. Ft. - Excluding Atrium; 52,235 Cu. Ft.

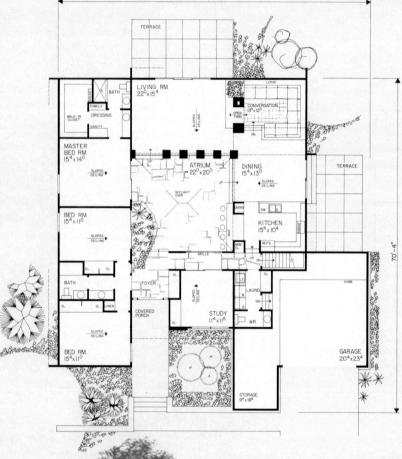

● The advantage of passive solar heating is a significant highlight of this contemporary design. The huge skylight over the atrium provides shelter during inclement weather, while permitting the enjoyment of plenty of natural light to the atrium below and surrounding areas. Whether open to the sky, or sheltered by a glass or translucent covering, the atrium becomes a cheerful spot and provides an abundance of natural light to its adjacent rooms. The stone floor will absorb an abundance of heat from the sun during the day and permit circulation of warm air to other areas at night. During the summer, shades afford protection from the sun without sacrificing the abundance of natural light and the feeling of spaciousness. Sloping ceilings highlight each of the major rooms, three bedrooms, formal living and dining and study. The conversation area between the two formal areas will really be something to talk about. The broad expanses of roof can accommodate solar panels should an active system be desired to supplement the passive features of this design.

Design 82831
1,758 Sq. Ft. - First Floor
1,247 Sq. Ft. - Second Floor
44,265 Cu. Ft.

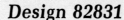

● You can incorporate energy-saving features into the elevation of this passive solar design to enable you to receive the most sunlight on your particular site. Multiple plot plans (included with the blueprints) illustrate which elevations should be solarized for different sites and which extra features can be incorporated. The features can include a greenhouse added to the family room, the back porch turned into a solarium or skylights installed over the entry.

Design 82882

2,832 Sq. Ft.; 59,635 Cu. Ft.

● This contemporary, one-story design should be oriented on a west-facing site if it is built in the northern regions of the country. The result will be minimal exposure to the cold northern winds during the winter. Study the north side of this plan. There is only one small window and it will be protected by the privacy wall. This means that the rooms on the opposite side of the house will have the desirable southern exposure. A westerly exposure for the living room will be most beneficial in many areas of the country. This plan reflects interesting living patterns and excellent indoor/outdoor relationships. Wide overhanging roofs, skylights, glass gables, vented walkways, wind-buffering privacy fences and 2x6 construction are among this design's energy oriented features.

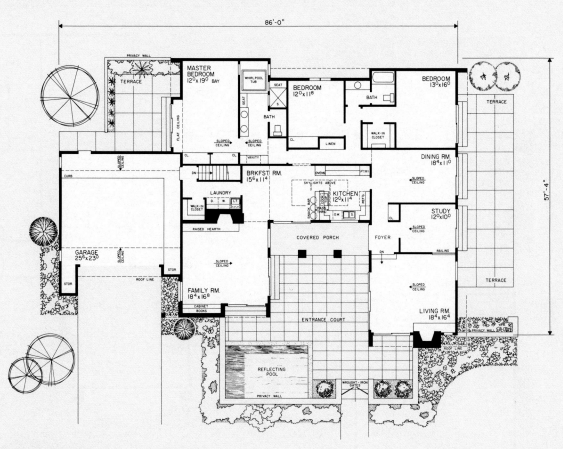

Design 82881 2,346 Sq. Ft.; 60,315 Cu. Ft.

● Energy-efficiency will be obtained in this unique, contemporary design. This plan has been designed for a south facing lot in the temperate zones. There is minimal window exposure on the north side of the house so the interior will be protected. The eastern side of the plan, on the other hand, will allow the morning sunlight to enter. As the sun travels from east to west, the various rooms will have light through windows, sliding glass doors or skylights. The garage acts as a buffer against the hot afternoon sun. The living areas are oriented to the front of the plan. They will benefit from the southern exposure during the cooler months. During the summer months, this area will be shielded from the high, hot summer sun by the overhanging roof. If you plan to build in the south, this house would be ideal for a north facing site. This results in a minimum amount of hot sun for the living areas and a maximum amount of protection from the sun on the rear, southern side of the house.

Design 82765 3,365 Sq. Ft.; 59,820 Cu. Ft.

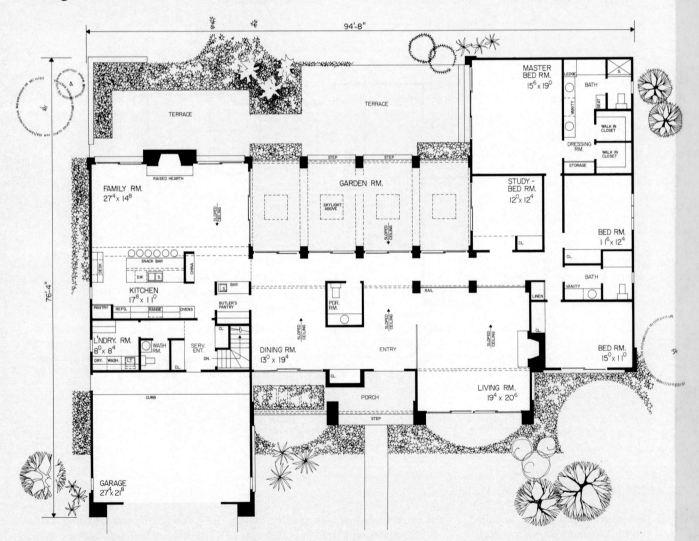

● This three (optional four) bedroom contemporary is very appealing. It offers living patterns that will add new dimensions to your everyday routine. You will enjoy all that natural light in the garden room from the skylights in the sloped ceiling. The sloped ceilings in the family room, dining room and living room add much spaciousness to this home. The efficient kitchen has many fine features including the island snack bar and work center, built-in desk, china cabinet and wet bar. Adjacent to the kitchen is a laundry room, wash room and stairs to the basement. Large areas are available for both formal and informal living. A raised hearth fireplace and sliding glass doors are in the informal family room. Another fireplace is centered in the front, formal living room.

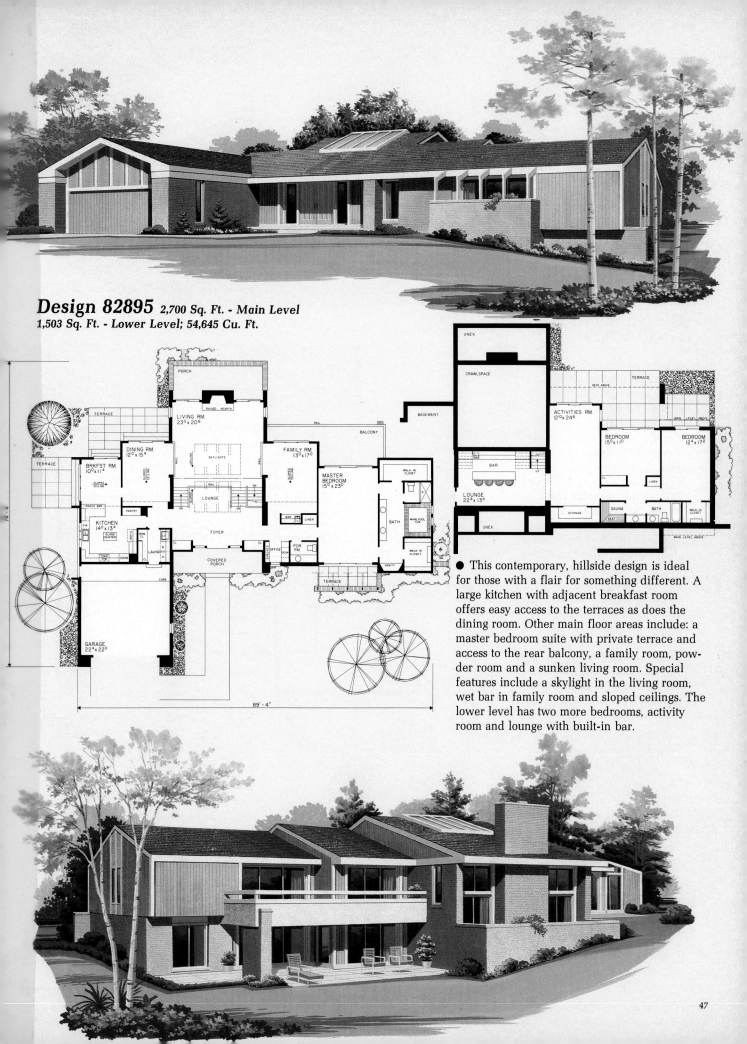

Design 82895 2,700 Sq. Ft. - Main Level
1,503 Sq. Ft. - Lower Level; 54,645 Cu. Ft.

● This contemporary, hillside design is ideal for those with a flair for something different. A large kitchen with adjacent breakfast room offers easy access to the terraces as does the dining room. Other main floor areas include: a master bedroom suite with private terrace and access to the rear balcony, a family room, powder room and a sunken living room. Special features include a skylight in the living room, wet bar in family room and sloped ceilings. The lower level has two more bedrooms, activity room and lounge with built-in bar.

Design 82861

2,499 Sq. Ft.; 29,100 Cu. Ft.

● Berming the earth against the walls of a structure prove to be very energy efficient. The earth protects the interior from the cold of the winter and the heat of the summer. Interior lighting will come from the large skylight over the garden room. Every room will benefit from this exposed area. The garden room will function as a multi-purpose area for the entire family. The living/dining room will receive light from two areas, the garden room and the wall of sliding glass doors to the outside. Family living will be served by the efficient floor plan. Three bedrooms and two full baths are clustered together. The kitchen is adjacent to the air-locked vestibule where the laundry and utility rooms are housed. The section is cut through the dining, garden and master bedroom facing the kitchen.

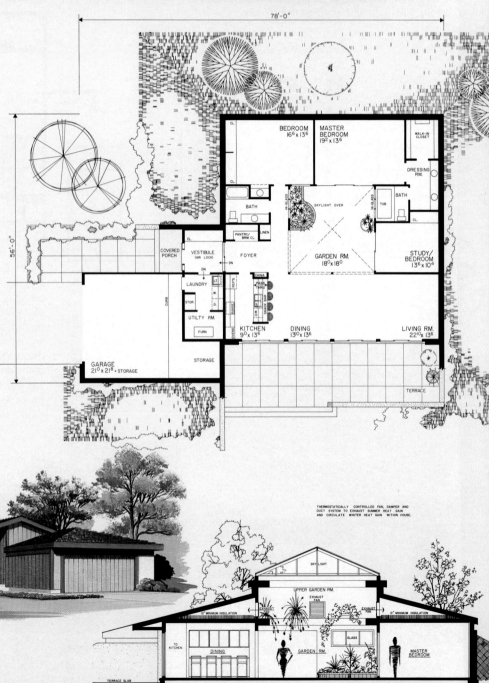

78'-0"

56'-0"

BEDROOM 16⁶ x 13⁶ MASTER BEDROOM 19² x 13⁶ WALK-IN CLOSET

CL. DRESSING RM.

BATH SKYLIGHT OVER TUB BATH CL.

PANTRY/ BRM. CL. LINEN

COVERED PORCH VESTIBULE (AIR LOCK) FOYER GARDEN RM. 18⁰ x 18⁰ STUDY/ BEDROOM/ 13⁶ x 10⁴

LAUNDRY CHINA

STOR. SNACK BAR

UTILITY RM. FURN. KITCHEN 9⁰ x 13⁶ DINING 13¹⁰ x 13⁶ LIVING RM. 22¹⁰ x 13⁶

GARAGE 21⁰ x 21⁶ + STORAGE STORAGE

TERRACE

THERMOSTATICALLY CONTROLLED FAN, DAMPER AND DUCT SYSTEM TO EXHAUST SUMMER HEAT GAIN AND CIRCULATE WINTER HEAT GAIN WITHIN HOUSE.

SKYLIGHT

UPPER GARDEN RM.

EXHAUST FAN

EXHAUST EXHAUST FAN

12" MINIMUM INSULATION 12" MINIMUM INSULATION

GLASS

TO KITCHEN DINING GARDEN RM. MASTER BEDROOM

TERRACE SLAB

SECTION

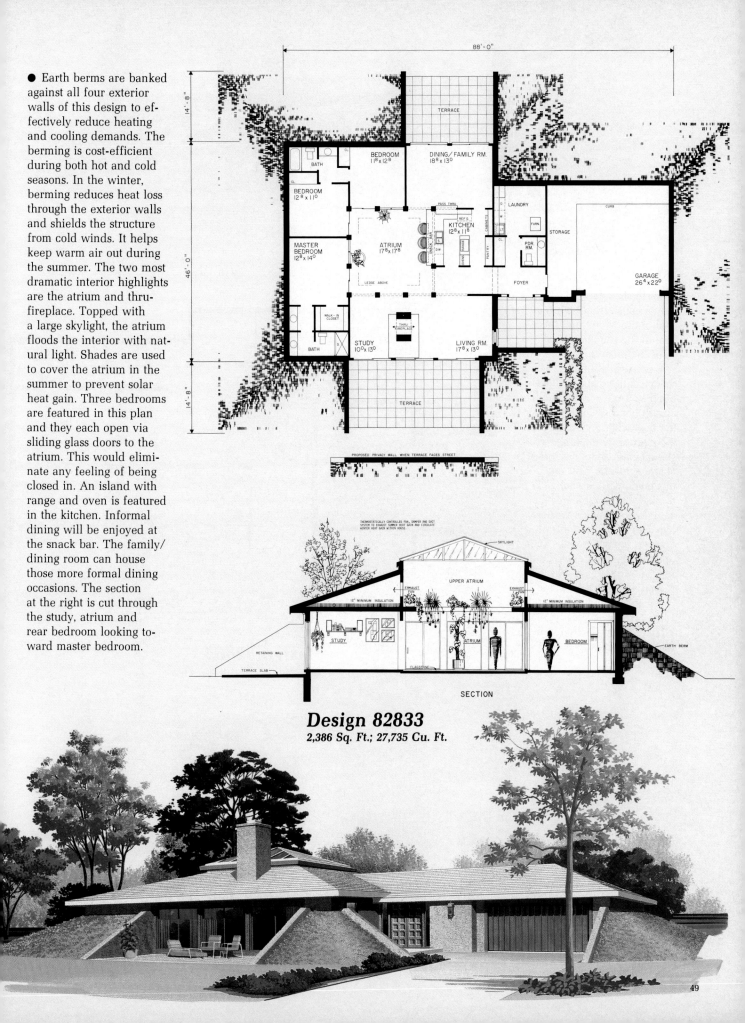

● Earth berms are banked against all four exterior walls of this design to effectively reduce heating and cooling demands. The berming is cost-efficient during both hot and cold seasons. In the winter, berming reduces heat loss through the exterior walls and shields the structure from cold winds. It helps keep warm air out during the summer. The two most dramatic interior highlights are the atrium and thru-fireplace. Topped with a large skylight, the atrium floods the interior with natural light. Shades are used to cover the atrium in the summer to prevent solar heat gain. Three bedrooms are featured in this plan and they each open via sliding glass doors to the atrium. This would eliminate any feeling of being closed in. An island with range and oven is featured in the kitchen. Informal dining will be enjoyed at the snack bar. The family/dining room can house those more formal dining occasions. The section at the right is cut through the study, atrium and rear bedroom looking toward master bedroom.

Design 82833
2,386 Sq. Ft.; 27,735 Cu. Ft.

● Earth shelters the interior of this house from both the cold of the winter and the heat of the summer. This three bedroom design has passive solar capabilities. The sun room, south facing for light, has a stone floor which will absorb heat. When needed, the heat will be circulated to the interior by opening the sliding glass doors or by mechanical means. Entrance to this home will be obtained through the vestibule or the garage. Both have a western exposure. A large, centrally located, skylight creates an open feeling and lights up the interior of this plan where the formal and informal living areas are located. The sun room contains 425 sq. ft. and 5,228 cu. ft. not included in totals to the right.

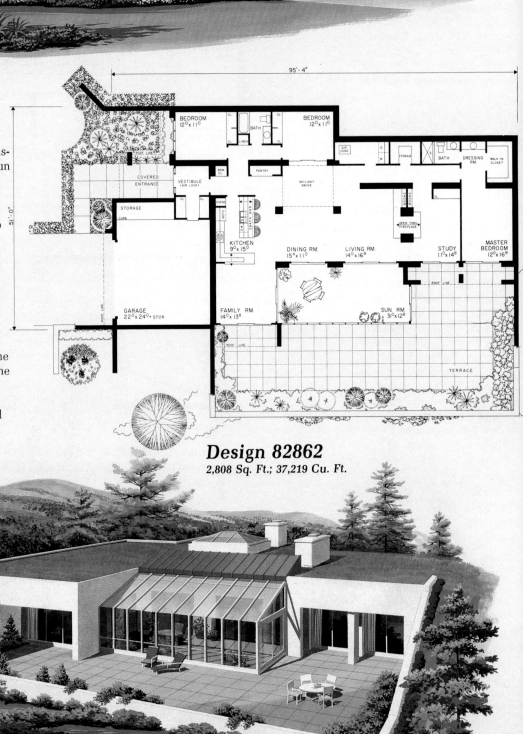

Design 82862
2,808 Sq. Ft.; 37,219 Cu. Ft.

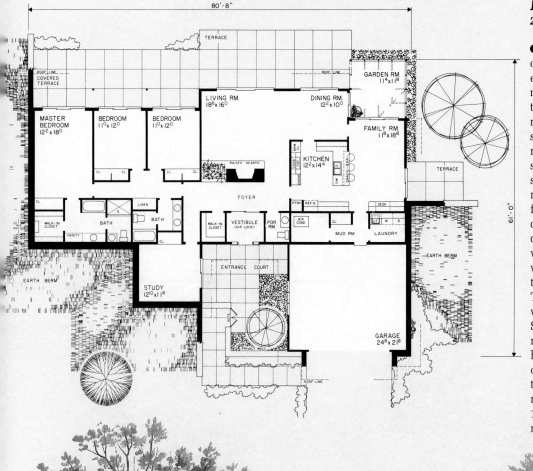

Design 82903
2,555 Sq. Ft.; 32,044 Cu. Ft.

● Earth berms on the sides of this house help it achieve energy-efficiency. The maximum amount of light enters this home by way of the many glass areas on the southern exposure. Every room in this plan, except the study, has the benefit of the southern sun. A garden room, tucked between the family and dining rooms, can be used for passive solar capabilities. A front privacy wall and the entrance court will shield the interior from the harsh northern winds. The air-locked vestibule also will be an energy saver. Summer heat gain will be reduced by the wide overhanging roof. The occupants of this home will appreciate the excellent interior planning. Garden room contains 144 sq. ft. and 1,195 cu. ft. not included in above totals.

Design 82860

2,240 Sq. Ft.; 27,685 Cu. Ft.

● Here is truly a unique home to satisfy your family's desires for something appealing and refreshing. This three bedroom home is also, the very embodiment of what's new and efficient in planning and technology. This is an excellent example of outstanding coordination of house structure, site, interior livability and the sun. Orienting this earth-sheltered house toward the south assures a warm, bright and cheerful interior. Major contributions to energy-efficiency result from the earth covered roof, the absence of northern wall exposure and the lack of windows on either end of the house. This means a retention of heat in the winter and cool air in the summer. An effective use of skylights provide the important extra measure of natural light to the interior. Sliding glass doors in the living and dining rooms also help bring the light to the indoors. This earth sheltered house makes no sacrifice of good planning and excellent, all 'round livability. The section is cut through the living room and the skylit hall looking toward the bedrooms.

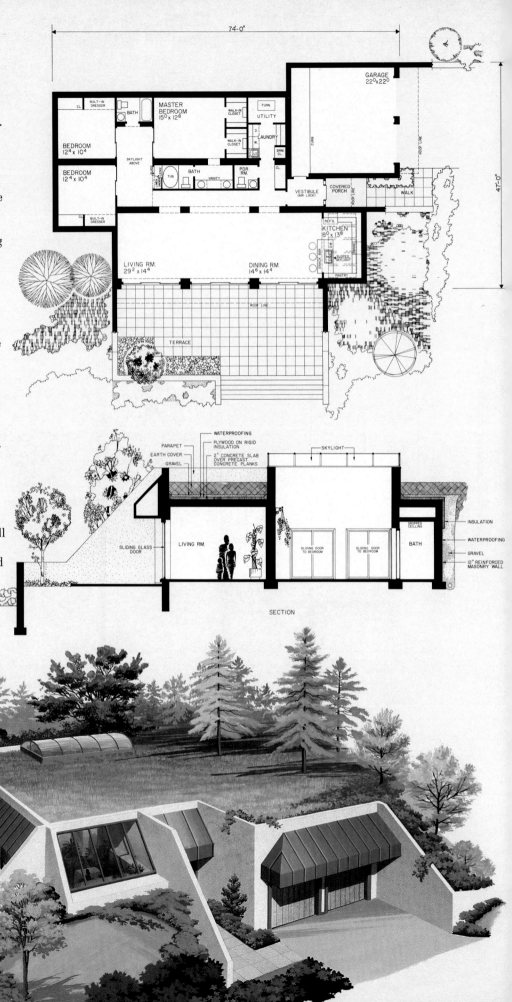

Design 82838 2,309 Sq. Ft.; 32,550 Cu. Ft.

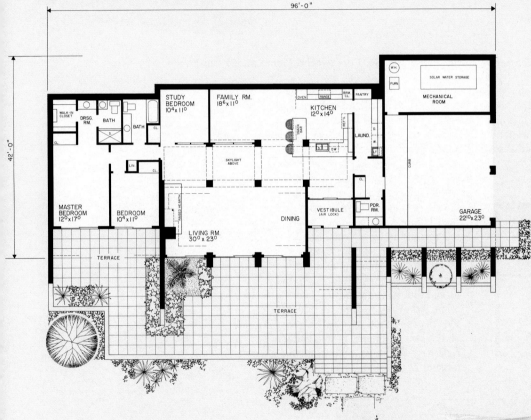

● Here is another dramatic earth sheltered home which will function with the sun like Design 82860. The spaciousness of the living area in this design is enhanced by the central location of the dramatic skylight. In addition to the passive solar heating gain for the living and bedroom areas, the impressively designed "mansard" roof effect lends itself to the installation of active solar heating panels. The illustration above shows panels only on the garage wing. Consultation with local solar heating experts will determine the effectiveness in your area of additional panels. A special room adjacent to the garage will accommodate mechanical equipment.

The section below is cut through the family and dining rooms, including the skylight, looking toward the fireplace wall.

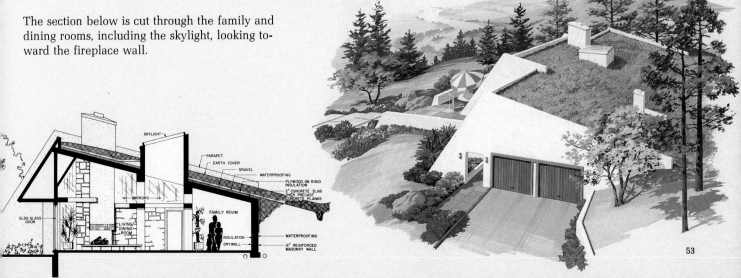

Design 82840 *1,529 Sq. Ft. - First Floor; 1,344 Sq. Ft. - Second Floor; 44,504 Cu. Ft.*

● This traditional, two-story design will keep you warm because it is super-insulated to shut out the cold. It is designed for cold climates and is so well insulated that it can be built facing any direction - even north. The key behind its energy-efficiency is its double exterior walls separated by R-33 insulation and a raised roof truss that insures ceiling insulation will extend to the outer wall. Front and rear air locks and triple-glazed, underscaled (24" wide) windows also contribute to the energy savings. The interior floor planning has a great deal to recommend it, too. Formal and informal living areas, plus a study! The interior kitchen area will be hard to beat. It has pass-thrus to the formal dining room and the family room. All of the sleeping facilities, four bedrooms and two baths, are on the second floor. The section at right describes the technical characteristics of this super-insulated house.

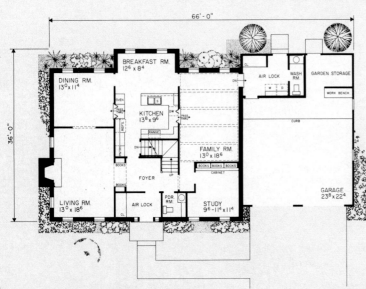

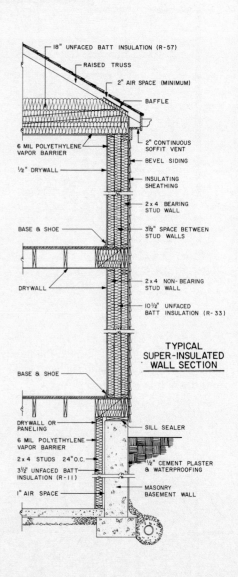

TYPICAL SUPER-INSULATED WALL SECTION

● Incorporated into the extremely popular basic one-story floor plan is a super-insulated structure. This means that it has double exterior walls separated by R-33 insulation and a raised roof truss that insures ceiling insulation will extend to the outer wall. More popularity is shown in the always popular Tudor facade. The design is a sure winner. Study the interior livability carefully. Enter the home through the air-locked vestibule to the foyer. To the left is the sleeping area. The three good-sized bedrooms are clustered together with the two full bathrooms. To the right of the foyer is the breakfast room, kitchen and stairs to the basement. Viewing the rear yard are the gathering and dining rooms. A raised hearth fireplace is located here. Study the technical details described in the wall section so you can better understand this super-insulated house.

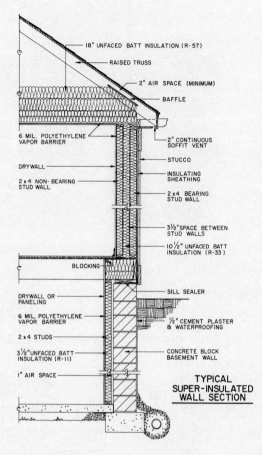

TYPICAL
SUPER-INSULATED
WALL SECTION

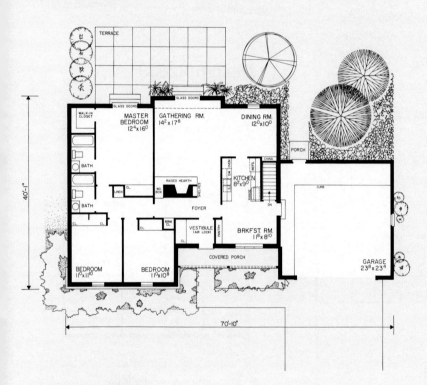

Design 82859
1,599 Sq. Ft.; 37,497 Cu. Ft.

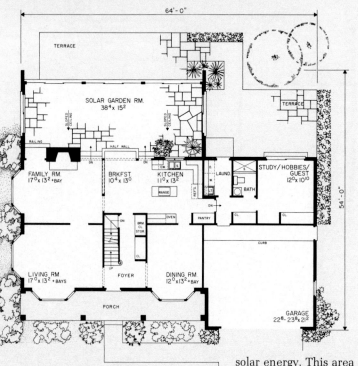

Design 82839

2,141 Sq. Ft. - First Floor
1,120 Sq. Ft. - Second Floor; 58,925 Cu. Ft.

● Bay windows highlight the front and side exteriors of this three-bedroom Colonial. For energy efficiency, this design has an enclosed garden room that collects free solar energy. This area opens to the family room, breakfast room and second floor master suite. The solar garden room includes 576 sq. ft. and 10,828 cu. ft. These figures are included in the above total.

Vacation Homes
Enjoying the Informality of Leisure Living

Design 82488 1,113 Sq. Ft. - First Floor; 543 Sq. Ft. - Second Floor; 36,055 Cu. Ft.

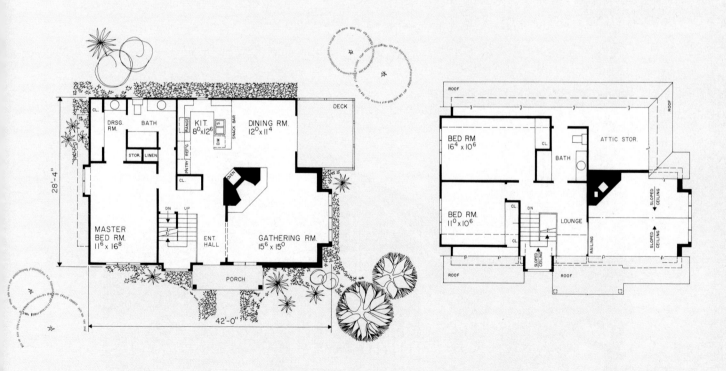

● A cozy cottage for the young at heart! Whether called upon to serve the young active family as a leisure-time retreat at the lake, or the retired couple as a quiet haven in later years, this charming design will perform well. As a year round second home, the up-stairs with its two sizable bedrooms, full bath and lounge area looking down into the gathering room below, will ideally accommodate the younger generation. When called upon to function as a retirement home, the second floor will cater to the visiting family members and friends. Also, it will be available for use as a home office, study, sewing room, music area, the pursuit of hobbies, etc. Of course, as an efficient, economical home for the young, growing family, this design will function well.

Design 81482 *1,008 Sq. Ft. - First Floor; 637 Sq. Ft. - Second Floor; 16,657 Cu. Ft.*

● Here's a chalet right from the pages of the travel folders. Whether the setting reflects the majestic beauty of a winter scene, or the tranquil splendor of a summer landscape, this design will serve its occupants well. In addition to the big bedrooms on the first floor, there are three more upstairs. The large master bedroom has a balcony which looks down into the lower wood deck. There are two full baths. The first floor bath is directly accessible from the outdoors. Note snack bar and pantry of the kitchen. Laundry area is adjacent to side door.

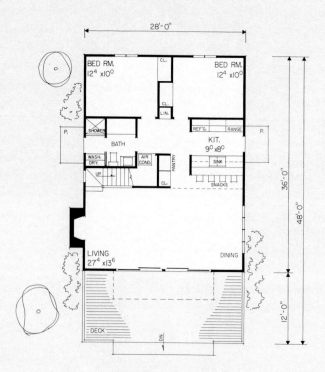

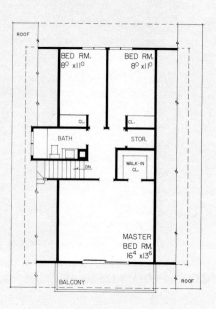

Design 82430 1,238 Sq. Ft. - First Floor; 648 Sq. Ft. - Second Floor; 18,743 Cu. Ft.

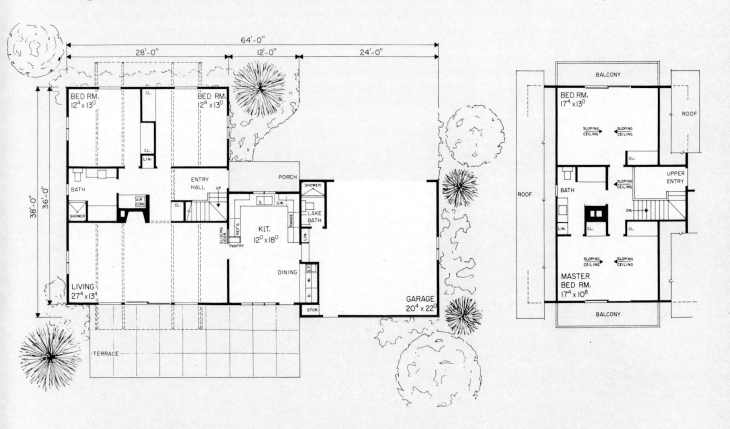

● Another Swiss chalet adaptation which will serve its occupants admirably during the four seasons of the year. The sun-drenched balcony and the terrace will be enjoyed as much by the skiers in the winter as by the swimmers in the summer. All the var-ious areas are equally outstanding. For sleeping, there are four big bedrooms. They are supported by two full baths – one has both tub and stall shower. For relaxation, there is the big living room. It has a fireplace and a large glass area to preserve the view. For eating, there is the U-shaped kitchen and its adja-cent dining area. Don't miss beamed ceilings of first floor, nor sloping ceil-ings of second floor. Note the position-ing of the lake bath adjacent to the kitchen entrance. Truly a strategic and convenient location.

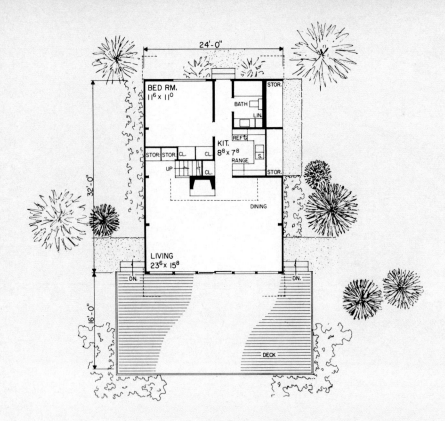

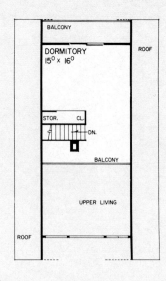

Design 81406
776 Sq. Ft. - First Floor
300 Sq. Ft. - Second Floor; 8,536 Cu. Ft.

● A spacious 23 foot by 15 foot living room is really something to talk about. And when it has a high, vaulted ceiling and a complete wall of windows it is even more noteworthy. Because of the wonderful glass area, the livability of the living room seems to spill right out onto the huge wood deck. In addition to the bedroom downstairs, there is the sizable dormitory upstairs for sleeping quite a crew. Sliding glass doors open onto the outdoor balcony from the dormitory. Don't miss the fireplace, the efficient kitchen and the numerous storage facilities. The outside storage units are accessible from just below the roof line and are great for all the recreational equipment. Don't be without the exceptional wood deck. It will make a vital contribution to your outdoor vacation enjoyment.

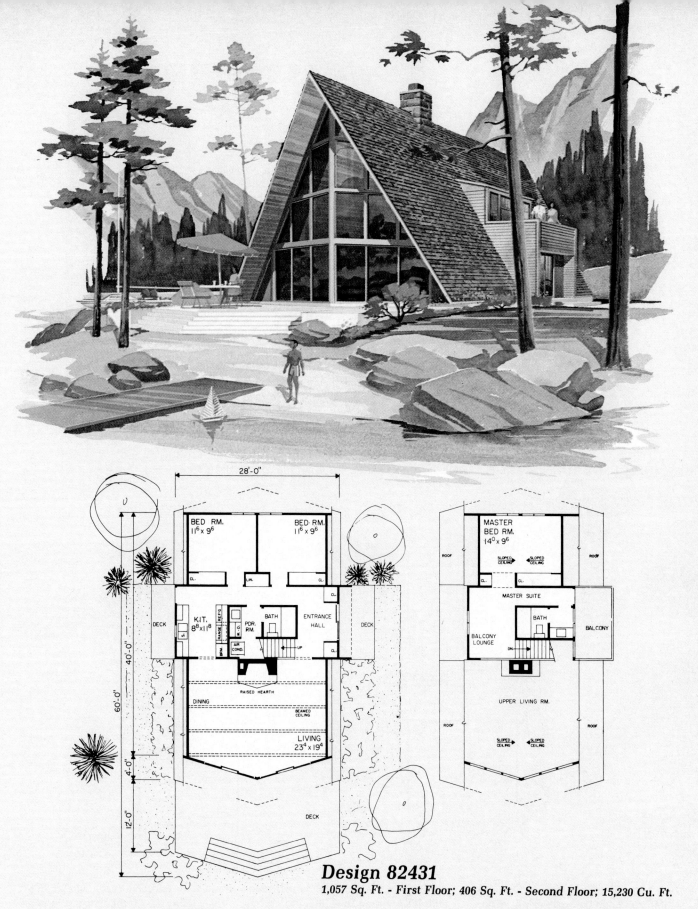

28'-0"

BED RM.
11⁶ x 9⁶

BED RM.
11⁶ x 9⁶

CL.   LIN.   CL.

CL.

DECK

KIT.
8⁸ x 11⁸

RANGE   REF'G.

W.C.   PDR. RM.

BATH

AIR COND.

ENTRANCE HALL

UP

CL.

DECK

RAISED HEARTH

DINING

BEAMED CEILING

LIVING
23⁴ x 19⁴

DECK

60'-0"

40'-0"

4'-0"

12'-0"

MASTER
BED RM.
14⁰ x 9⁶

ROOF   ROOF

SLOPED CEILING   SLOPED CEILING

CL.   CL.

MASTER SUITE

BALCONY LOUNGE

BATH

BALCONY

DN.

UPPER LIVING RM.

ROOF   ROOF

SLOPED CEILING   SLOPED CEILING

Design 82431
1,057 Sq. Ft. - First Floor; 406 Sq. Ft. - Second Floor; 15,230 Cu. Ft.

● A favorite everywhere – the A-frame vacation home. Its popularity is easily discernable at first glance. The stately appearance is enhanced by the soaring roof lines and the dramatic glass areas. Inside, the breathtaking beauty of outstanding architectural detailing also is apparent. The high ceiling of the living room slopes and has exposed beams. The second floor master suite is a great feature. Observe the raised hearth fireplace and the outdoor balcony. This outdoor spot certainly will be a quiet perch for sun bathing on a warm afternoon.

Design 82466 1,240 Sq. Ft. – First Floor; 815 Sq. Ft. – Second Floor; 19,974 Cu. Ft.

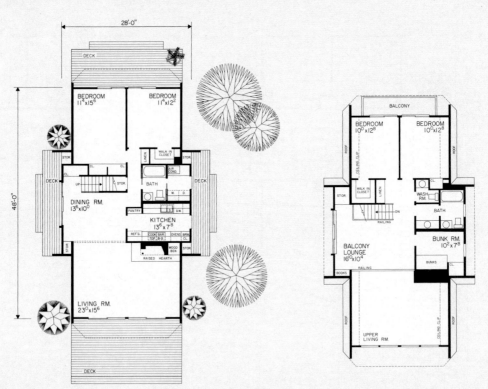

● You will, indeed, find it difficult to improve upon the exterior distinction and the interior livability offered by this truncated A-frame. While the basic dimension of the structure is 24 feet in width, its depth is 48 feet. Cleverly planned within the confines of these dimensions, this home is loaded with leisure-time livability. Fine provisions are made for the fullest enjoyment of the outdoors from within. In addition to the decks for the living and dining rooms, there is the deck servicing the first floor bedrooms. The second floor bedrooms also have an outdoor living area – the balcony. A combination of these features will guarantee enjoyment. Be sure you don't miss the bunk room, two full baths, extra wash room, mud room and lounge/balcony of the second floor.

Design 82467 720 Sq. Ft. – First Floor; 483 Sq. Ft. – Second Floor; 10,512 Cu. Ft.

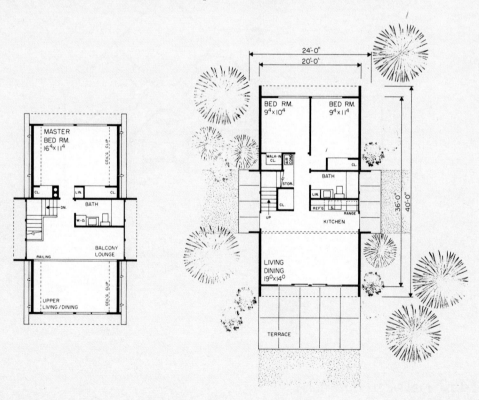

● Here is another dramatic variation of the popular A-frame. The roof modifications result in a structure that is somewhat similar to the configuration of the mansard roof. The utilization of the form with those large glass areas produces a blending of traditional and contemporary design features. The more nearly vertical side walls of this type of a design results in a greater amount of space inside than offered by the usual A-frame. Observe the great amount of livability in this plan. In addition to the two downstairs bedrooms, there is an upstairs master bedroom. Also there is a second full bath and a balcony lounge overlooking the living room. When needed, the lounge area could accommodate a couple of cots for weekend vacationers. Count the storage facilities.

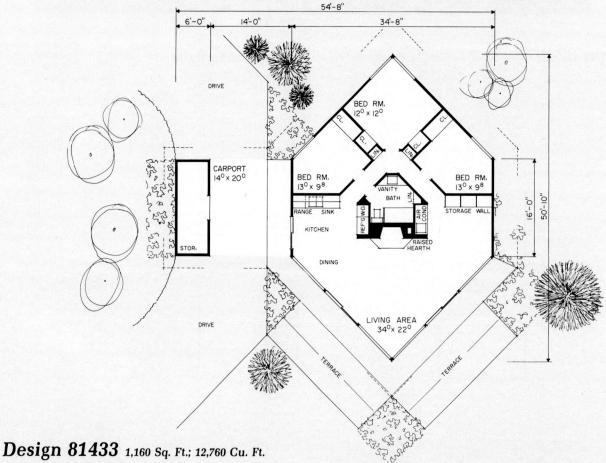

Design 81433 *1,160 Sq. Ft.; 12,760 Cu. Ft.*

● This hexagonal vacation, or leisure-time, home surely will prove to be a delightful haven away from the conventions of everyday living. Like a breath of fresh air, its uniqueness will make the hours spent in and around this second home memorable ones, indeed. The floor plan, in spite of its shape, reflects a wise and economical use of space. The spacious interior features a raised hearth fireplace, abundant storage facilities, a bathroom vanity and a combination washer-dryer space. Then, there is the attached carport and its bulk storage area for recreational and garden equipment. The wide, overhanging roof provides protection from the rays of the hot summer sun. This will be a great house for your family to enjoy the beauty of the countryside.

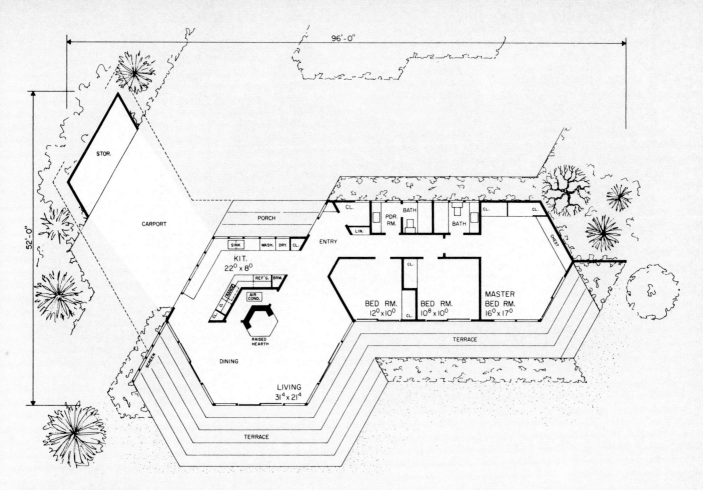

Design 81453 1,476 Sq. Ft.; 13,934 Cu. Ft.

● An exciting design, unusual in character, yet fun to live in. This frame home with its vertical siding and large glass areas has as its dramatic focal point a hexagonal living area which gives way to interesting angles. The large living area features sliding glass doors where traffic may pass to the terrace. This terrace stretches across the entire length of the house. The wide overhanging roof projects over the terrace and results in a large covered area outside the sliding doors of the master bedroom. The sloping ceilings converge above the unique open fireplace which has a copper hood. The drive approach and the angles of the covered front entrance make this an eye-catching design. Surely an extraordinary design for a new lease on living for summer or winter fun.

Design 82439 1,312 Sq. Ft.; 17,673 Cu. Ft.

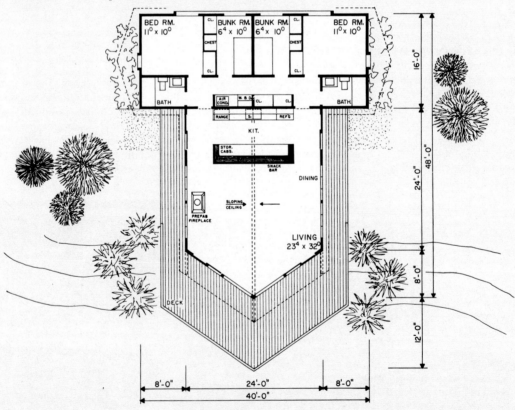

● A wonderfully organized plan with an exterior that will surely command the attention of each and every passerby. And what will catch the eye? Certainly the roof lines and the pointed glass gable end wall will be noticed immediately. The delightful deck will be quickly noticed, too. Inside a visitor will be thrilled by the spaciousness of the huge living room. The ceilings slope upward to the exposed ridge beam. A free-standing fireplace will make its contribution to a cheerful atmosphere. The kitchen is separated from the living area by a three foot high snack bar with cupboards below servicing the kitchen. What could improve upon the sleeping zone when it has two bedrooms, two bunk rooms, two full baths, two built-in chests and fine closet space?

Design 82417 1,520 Sq. Ft.; 19,952 Cu. Ft.

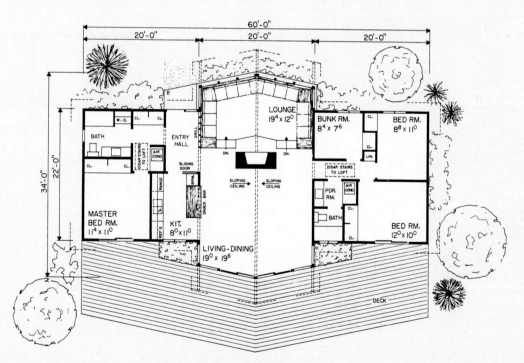

● Have you ever seen a vacation home design that is anything quite like this one? Probably not. The picturesque exterior is dominated by a projecting gable with its wide overhanging roof acting as a dramatic sun visor for the wonderfully large glass area below.

Effectively balancing this 20 foot center section are two 20 foot wings. Inside, and below the high, sloping, beamed ceiling is the huge living area. In addition to the living-dining area, there is the spacious sunken lounge. This pleasant area has a built-in seat-

ing arrangement and a cozy fireplace. The kitchen is efficient and handy to the snack bar and dining area. The parents' and children's sleeping areas are separated and each has a full bath. The large deck is accessible from sliding glass doors.

Design 82455
864 Sq. Ft. - Upper Level
864 Sq. Ft. - Lower Level; 16,934 Cu. Ft.

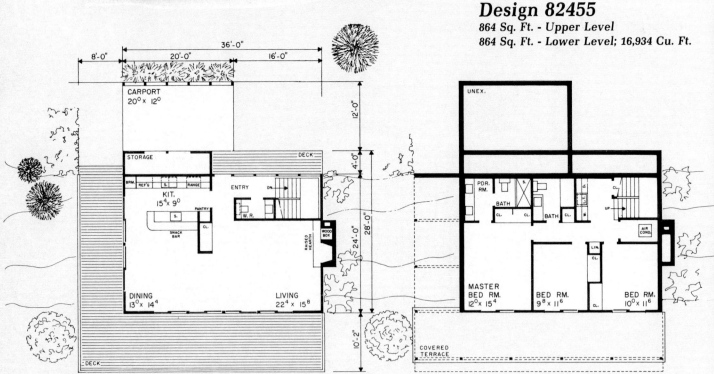

● What delightful vacation living experiences will be in store for the owners and guests of this great second home. Designed for a sloping site, the lakeside elevation has both the upper and lower levels completely exposed for the fullest enjoyment of indoor-outdoor living patterns. The wooden deck, which runs the full length of two sides of the house, is but a step from the upper level living areas. The covered terrace is readily accessible from the lower level bedrooms. The carport with its bulk storage room is located on the same grade as the upper level. The wonderful living-dining area is 35 feet in length. It features sliding glass doors and a strategically placed raised hearth fireplace. Don't miss the snack bar, the wash room, the two full baths and the powder room.

Design 82457 *1,288 Sq. Ft.; 13,730 Cu. Ft.*

● Leisure living will indeed be graciously experienced in this hip-roofed second home. Not counting the clipped corner, it is a perfect square measuring 36 x 36 feet. The 23 foot square living room enjoys a great view of the surrounding environment by virtue of the expanses of glass. The wide overhanging roof affords protection from the sun. The "open planning" adds to the spaciousness of the interior. The focal point is the raised hearth fireplace. The three bedrooms are serviced by two full baths which are also accessible to other areas. The kitchen, looking out upon the water, will be a delight to work in. Observe the carport, the big bulk storage room and the dressing room with its stall shower. This is definitely great planning for a leisure-time second home.

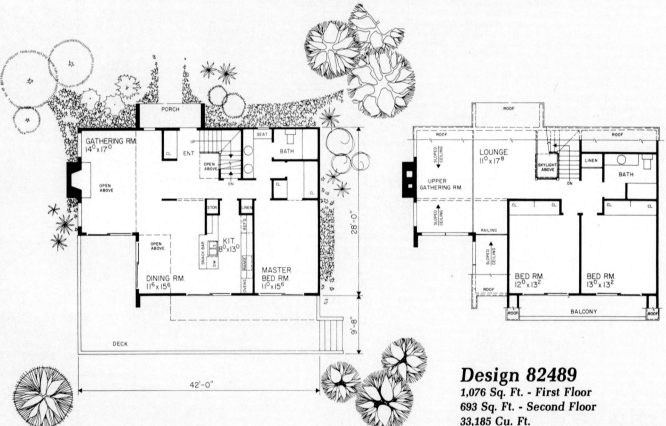

Design 82489
1,076 Sq. Ft. - First Floor
693 Sq. Ft. - Second Floor
33,185 Cu. Ft.

● Outdoors-oriented families will appreciate the dramatic sliding glass doors and the sweeping decks that make this contemporary perfect. The plan of the first floor features a spacious two-story gathering room with sloping ceiling, a large fireplace and access to the large deck which runs the full length of the house. Also having direct access to the deck is the dining room which is half-open to the second floor above. A snack bar divides the dining room from the compact kitchen. The master bedroom is outstanding with its private bath, walk-in closet and sliding glass door. The second floor is brightened by a skylight and houses two bedrooms, lounge and full bath.

Design 82485 1,108 Sq. Ft. - Main Level
983 Sq. Ft. - Lower Level; 21,530 Cu. Ft.

● This hillside vacation home gives the appearance of being a one-story from the road. However, since it is built off the edge of a slope, the rear exterior is a full two-story structure. Notice the projecting deck and how it shelters the terrace. Each of the generous glass areas is protected from the summer sun by the overhangs and the extended walls. The clerestory windows of the front exterior provide natural light to the center of the plan.

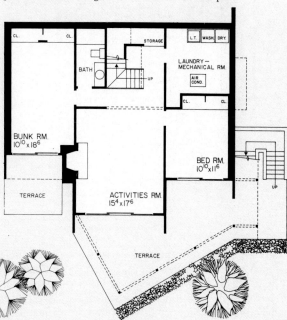

GARAGE 21⁴x21⁸

CURB

PORCH

WALK-IN CLOSET

DRESSING RM.

ENTRY

DN

CL.

BATH

B.CL.

KITCHEN 9⁴x5⁶

RANGE

REF'G

S. DW.

NOOK 9⁴x8⁰

PANTRY

CLERESTORY ABOVE

MASTER BED RM. 11⁸x14⁰

BALCONY

SLOPED CEILING

DINING RM. 12⁰x11⁶

DN

GATHERING RM. 15⁴x17⁴

DECK

54'-0"

40'-0"

CL.

CL.

STORAGE

L.T. WASH. DRY.

BATH

UP

LAUNDRY – MECHANICAL RM.

AIR COND.

CL.

CL.

BUNK RM. 10¹⁰x18⁶

BED RM. 10¹⁰x11⁶

UP

TERRACE

ACTIVITIES RM. 15⁴x17⁶

TERRACE

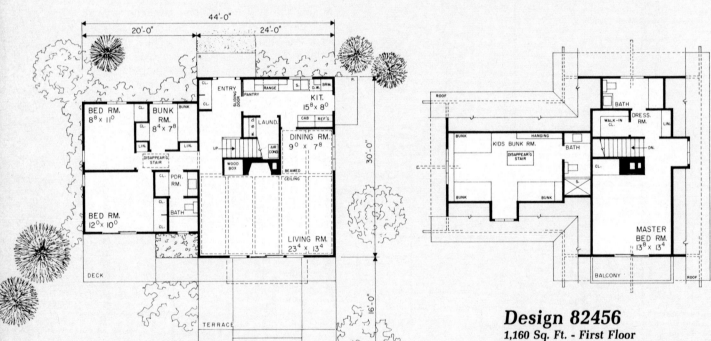

Design 82456

1,160 Sq. Ft. - First Floor
840 Sq. Ft. - Second Floor; 17,510 Cu. Ft.

● Here's how your Swiss chalet adaptation may look in the winter. Certainly an appealing design whatever the season. A delightful haven for skiers, fishermen and hunters alike. As for sleeping facilities, you'll really be able to pack 'em in. The first floor has two bedrooms plus a room which will take a double bunk. Across the hall is the compartment bath. A disappearing stair unit leads to the children's bunk room. The placement of single bunks or cots will permit the sleeping of three or four more. A bath with stall shower is nearby. The master bedroom suite is complete with walk-in closet, dressing room and private bath and opens onto the balcony. There is plenty of space in the L-shaped living-dining area with wood box and fireplace to accommodate the whole gang.

ALL the "TOOLS" you and your builder need. . .

. . . to, first select an exterior and a floor plan for your new house that satisfy your tastes and your family's living patterns . . .

. . . then, to review the blueprints in great detail and obtain a construction cost figure . . . also, to price out the structural materials required to build . . . and, finally, to review and decide upon the specifications to which your home is to be built. Truly, an invaluable set of "tools" to launch your home planning and building programs.

1. THE PLAN BOOKS

Home Planners' unique Design Category Series makes it easy to look at and study only the types of designs for which you and your family have an interest. Each of five plan books features a specific type of home, namely: 1½ and 2-Story, One-Story Over 2000 Sq. Ft., One-Story Under 2000 Sq. Ft., Multi-Levels and Vacation Homes. In addition to the convenient Design Category Series, there is an impressive selection of other current titles. While the home plans featured in these books are also to be found in the Design Category Series, they, too, are edited for those with special tastes and requirements. Your family will spend many enjoyable hours reviewing the delightfully designed exteriors and the practical floor plans. Surely your home or office library should include a selection of these popular plan books. Your complete satisfaction is guaranteed.

2. THE CONSTRUCTION BLUEPRINTS

There are blueprints available for each of the designs published in Home Planners' current plan books. Depending upon the size, the style and the type of home, each set of blueprints consists of from five to ten large sheets. Only by studying the blueprints is it possible to give complete and final consideration to the proper selection of a design for your next home. The blueprints provide the opportunity for all family members to familiarize themselves with the features of all exterior elevations, interior elevations and details, all dimensions, special built-in features and effects. They also provide a full understanding of the materials to be used and/or selected. The low-cost of our blueprints makes it possible and indeed, practical, to study in detail a number of different sets of blueprints before deciding upon which design to build.

3. THE MATERIAL LIST

A list of materials is an integral part of the plan package. It comprises the last sheet of each set of blueprints and serves as a handy reference during the period of construction. Of course, at the pricing and the material ordering stages, it is indispensable.

4. THE SPECIFICATION OUTLINE

Each order for blueprints is accompanied by one Specification Outline. You and your builder will find this a time-saving tool when deciding upon your own individual specifications. An important reference document should you wish to write your own specifications.

The Design Category Series

360 TWO STORY HOMES

English Tudors, Early American Salt Boxes, Gambrels, Farmhouses, Southern Colonials, Georgians, French Mansards, Contemporaries. Interesting floor plans for both small and large families. Efficient kitchens, 2 to 6 bedrooms, family rooms, libraries, extra baths, mud rooms. Homes for all budgets.

1.

288 Pages, $6.95

150 1½ STORY HOMES

Cape Cod, Williamsburg, Georgian, Tudor and Contemporary versions. Low budget and country-estate feature sections. Expandable family plans. Formal and informal living and dining areas along with gathering rooms. Spacious, country kitchens. Indoor-outdoor livability with covered porches and functional terraces.

2.

128 Pages, $3.95

210 ONE STORY HOME: OVER 2,000 Sq. Ft.

All popular styles. Includi: Spanish, Western, Tudo: French, and other tradition versions. Contemporarie Gracious, family living pa terns. Sunken living room master bedroom suites, at ums, courtyards, pools. Fir indoor-outdoor living rela tionships. For modest i country-estate budgets.

3.

192 Pages, $4.95

315 ONE STORY HOMES UNDER 2,000 Sq. Ft.

A great selection of traditional and contemporary exteriors for medium and restricted budgets. Efficient, practical floor plans. Gathering rooms, formal and informal living and dining rooms, mud rooms, indoor-outdoor livability. Economically built homes. Designs with bonus space livability for growing families.

4.

192 Pages, $4.95

215 MULTI-LEVEL HOMES

For new dimensions in family living. A captivating variety of exterior styles, exciting floor plans for flat and sloping sites. Exposed lower levels. Balconies, decks. Plans for the active family. Upper level lounges, excellent bath facilities. Sloping ceilings. Functional outdoor terraces. For all building budgets.

5.

192 Pages, $4.95

223 VACATION HOME:

Features A-Frames, Chalet Hexagons, economical rectan gles. One and two stories plu multi-levels. Lodges for yea 'round livability. From 480 t 3238 sq. ft. Cottages sleeping to 22. For flat or sloping site Spacious, open planning. Ove 600 illustrations. 120 Pages i full color. Cluster home selection. For lakeshore o woodland leisure living.

6.

176 Pages, $4.95

The Exterior Style Series

330 EARLY AMERICAN PLANS

Our new *Essential Guide to Early American Home Plans* traces Early American architecture from our Colonial Past to Traditional styles popular today with a written history of designs and colorful sections devoted to styles. Many of our designs are patterned after historic homes.

7.

304 Pages, $9.95

335 CONTEMPORARY HOME PLANS

Our new *Essential Guide to Contemporary Home Plans* offers a colorful directory to modern architecture, including a history of American Contemporary styling and more than 335 home plans of all sizes and popular designs. 304 colorful pages!

8.

304 Pages, $9.95

135 ENGLISH TUDOR HOMES

and other Popular Family Plans is a favorite of many The current popularity of the English Tudor home design is phenomenal. Here is a book which is loaded with Tudors for all budgets. There are one-story, 1½ and two-story designs, plus multi-levels and hillsides from 1,176 to 3,849 sq. ft. There is a special 20 page section of Early American Adaptations.

9.

104 Pages, $3.95

The Budget Series

175 LOW BUDGET HOMES

A special selection of home designs for the modest or restricted building budget. An excellent variety of Traditional and Contemporary designs. One-story, 1½ and two-story and split-level homes. Three, four and five bedrooms. Family rooms, extra baths, formal and informal dining rooms. Basement and non-basement designs. Attached garages an covered porches.

13.

96 Pages, $2.95

165 AFFORDABLE HOME PLANS

This outstanding book was specially edited with a wide selection of houses and plans for those with a medium building budget. While none of these designs are considered low-cost; neither do they require an unlimited budget to build. Square footages range from 1,428. Exteriors of Tudor, French, Early American, Spanish and Contemporary are included.

14.

112 Pages, $2.95

142 HOME DESIGNS FOR EXPANDED BUILDING BUDGETS

A family's ability to finance and need for a larger home grows as its size and income increases. This selection highlights designs which house an average square footage of 2,551. One-story plans average 2,069; two-stories, 2,735; multi-levels, 2,825. Spacious homes featuring raised hearth fireplaces, open planning and efficient kitchens.

15.

112 Pages, $2.95

Other Current Titles

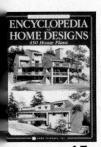

ENCYCLOPEDIA - 450 PLANS

For those who wish to review and study perhaps the largest selection of designs available in a single volume. Varying exterior styles, plus interesting and practical floor plans for all building budgets. Formal, informal living patterns; indoor-outdoor livability; small, growing and large family facilities.

15.

320 Pages, $9.95

244 HOUSE PLANS FOR BETTER LIVING

Special 40th Anniversary Edition with over 650 illustrations. Sectionalized to highlight special interest groups of designs. A fine introduction to our special interest titles. All styles, sizes, and types of homes are represented.

16.

192 Pages $3.50

255 HOME DESIGNS FOR FAMILY LIVING

In addition to the plans that cater to a variety of family living patterns and budgets, there are special sections on vacation homes, earth-sheltered homes, sun-oriented living, and shared livability. One, 1½, two-story, and multi-level designs.

17.

192 Pages, $3.50

COLOR PORTFOLIO - 310 DESIGNS

An expanded full-color guide to our most popular Early American, Spanish, French, Tudor, Contemporary, and modern Trend home designs. 310 home plans of all popular styles and sizes. Includes energy-efficient designs. Plans for varying building budgets. One, 1½, two-story, and split-level designs for all terrain. This is our largest full-color book with our newest trend-setting designs and other favorites. It's must reading for the serious home planner.

18.

288 Pages in Full Color, $12.95

136 SPANISH & WESTERN HOME DESIGNS

Stucco exteriors, arches, tile roofs, wide-overhangs, courtyards and rambling ranches are characteristics which make this design selection distinctive. These sun-country designs highlight indoor-outdoor relationships. Solar oriented livability is featured. Their appeal is not limited to the Southwest region of our country.

10.

120 Pages, $2.95

PLAN BOOKS are a valuable tool for anyone who plans to build a new home. After you have selected a home design that satisfies your list of requirements, you can order blueprints for further study.

115 HOME DESIGNS FOR UNLIMITED BUILDING BUDGETS

This book will appeal to those with large families, maybe live-in relatives, those with large building sites, and the desire and wherewithal to satisfy all the family needs, plus most of their wants. The upscale designs in this portfolio average 3,132 square feet. One-story designs average 2,796 sq. ft.; 1½-story, 3,188 sq. ft.; two-story, 3,477 sq. ft.; multi-level, 3,532 sq. ft. Truly designs for elegant living.

14.

112 Pages, $2.95

HOME PLANNERS, INC.

Dept. BK, 23761 Research Drive
Farmington Hills, Michigan 48024

Please mail me the following:

THE DESIGN CATEGORY SERIES - A great series of books specially edited by design type and size. Each book features interesting sections to further enhance the study of design styles, sizes and house types. A fine addition to the home or office library. Complete collection - over 1250 designs.

1. _____ 360 Two Story Homes @ $6.95 ea. .... $_____
2. _____ 150 1½ Story Homes @ $3.95 ea. .... $_____
3. _____ 210 One Story Homes - Over 2,000 Sq. Ft. @ $4.95 ea. . $_____
4. _____ 315 One Story Homes - Under 2,000 Sq. Ft. @ $4.95 ea. $_____
5. _____ 215 Multi-Level Homes @ $4.95 ea. .... $_____
6. _____ 223 Vacation Homes @ $4.95 ea. .... $_____

OTHER CURRENT TITLES - The interesting series of plan books listed below have been edited to appeal to various style preferences and budget considerations. The majority of the designs highlighted in these books also may be found in the Design Category Series.

The Exterior Style Series-
7. _____ 330 Early American Home Plans @ $9.95 ea. .... $_____
8. _____ 335 Contemporary Home Plans @ $9.95 ea. .... $_____
9. _____ 135 English Tudor Homes @ $3.95 ea. .... $_____
10. _____ 136 Spanish & Western Home Designs @ $2.95 ea. .... $_____

The Budget Series-
11. _____ 175 Low Budget Homes @ $2.95 ea. .... $_____
12. _____ 165 Affordable Home Plans @ $2.95 ea. .... $_____
13. _____ 142 Home Designs for Expanded Budgets @ $2.95 ea. . $_____
14. _____ 115 Home Designs for Unlimited Budgets @ $2.95 ea. . $_____

Other Current Titles-
15. _____ Encyclopedia of Home Designs - 450 Designs @ $9.95 ea. $_____
16. _____ 244 House Plans for Better Living @ $3.50 ea. .... $_____
17. _____ 255 Home Designs for Family Living @ $3.50 ea. ..... $_____

Full Color Book-
18. _____ Color Portfolio of Houses & Plans - 310 Designs @ $12.95 ea. $_____

Sub Total $_____
Michigan Residents
kindly add 4% sales tax $_____
TOTAL-Check enclosed $_____

Your order will be processed
and shipped within 48 hours

MAIL TODAY
SATISFACTION GUARANTEED!

Please Print

Name _____

Address _____

City _____ State _____ Zip _____

In Canada Mail To: Home Planners, Inc., 20 Cedar St. North,
Kitchener, Ontario N2H 2W8   108BK

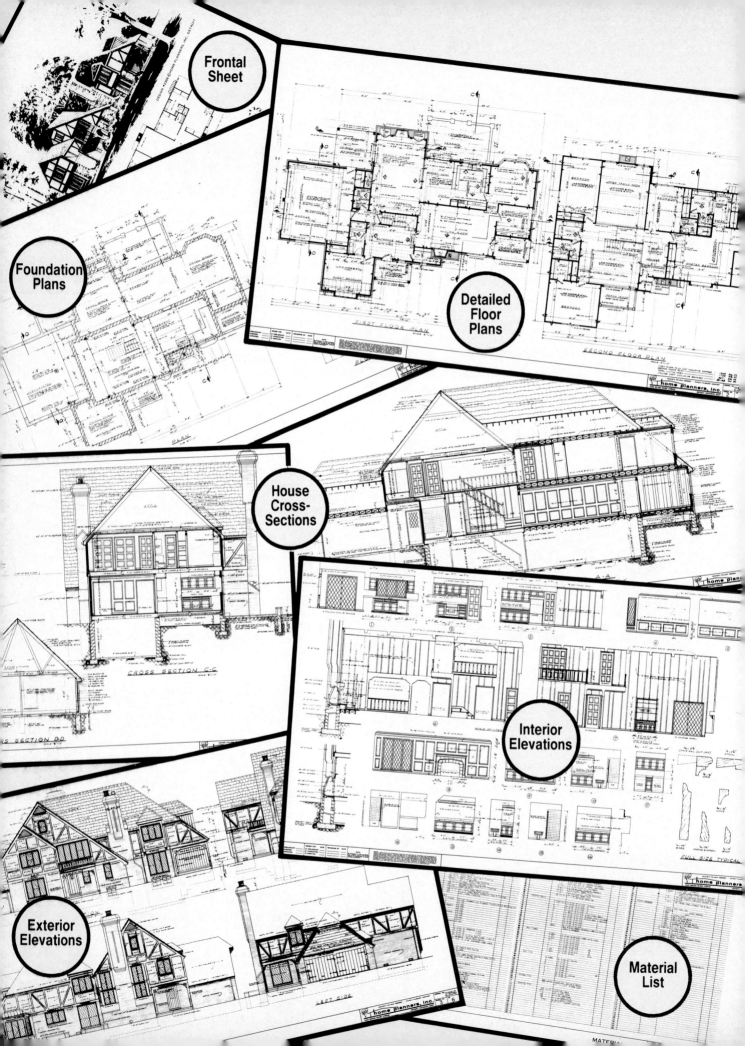

Frontal Sheet

Foundation Plans

Detailed Floor Plans

House Cross-Sections

Interior Elevations

Exterior Elevations

Material List

The Blueprints. . .

1. FRONTAL SHEET.
Artist's landscaped sketch of the exterior and ink-line floor plans are on the frontal sheet of each set of blueprints.

2. FOUNDATION PLAN.
¼" Scale basement and foundation plan. All necessary notations and dimensions. Plot plan diagram for locating house on building site.

3. DETAILED FLOOR PLAN.
¼" Scale first and second floor plans with complete dimensions. Cross-section detail keys. Diagrammatic layout of electrical outlets and switches.

4. HOUSE CROSS-SECTIONS.
Large scale sections of foundation, interior and exterior walls, floors and roof details for design and construction control.

5. INTERIOR ELEVATIONS.
Large scale interior details of the complete kitchen cabinet design, bathrooms, powder room, laundry, fireplaces, paneling, beam ceilings, built-in cabinets, etc.

6. EXTERIOR ELEVATIONS.
¼" Scale exterior elevation drawings of front, rear, and both sides of the house. All exterior materials and details are shown to indicate the complete design and proportions of the house.

7. MATERIAL LIST.
Complete lists of all materials required for the construction of the house as designed are included in each set of blueprints.

THIS BLUEPRINT PACKAGE
will help you and your family take a major step forward in the final appraisal and planning of your new home. Only by spending many enjoyable and informative hours studying the numerous details included in the complete package, will you feel sure of, and comfortable with, your commitment to build your new home. To assure successful and productive consultation with your builder and/or architect, reference to the various elements of the blueprint package is a must. The blueprints, material list and specification outline will save much consultation time and expense. Don't be without them.

The Material List. . .

With each set of blueprints you order you will receive a material list. Each list shows you the quantity, type and size of the non-mechanical materials required to build your home. It also tells you where these materials are used. This makes the blueprints easy to understand.

Influencing the mechanical requirements are geographical differences in availability of materials, local codes, methods of installation and individual preferences. Because of these factors, your local heating, plumbing and electrical contractors can supply you with necessary material take-offs for their particular trades.

Material lists simplify your material ordering and enable you to get quicker price quotations from your builder and material dealer. Because the material list is an integral part of each set of blueprints, it is not available separately.

Among the materials listed:

• Masonry, Veneer & Fireplace • Framing Lumber • Roofing & Sheet Metal • Windows & Door Frames • Exterior Trim & Insulation • Tile Work, Finish Floors • Interior Trim, Kitchen Cabinets • Rough & Finish Hardware

The Specification Outline. . .

This fill-in type specification lists over 150 phases of home construction from excavating to painting and includes wiring, plumbing, heating and air-conditioning. It consists of 16 pages and will prove invaluable for specifying to your builder the exact materials, equipment and methods of construction you want in your new home. One Specification Outline is included free with each order for blueprints. Additional Specification Outlines are available at $3.00 each.

CONTENTS
• General Instructions, Suggestions and Information • Excavating and Grading • Masonry and Concrete Work • Sheet Metal Work • Carpentry, Millwork, Roofing, and Miscellaneous Items • Lath and Plaster or Drywall Wallboard • Schedule for Room Finishes • Painting and Finishing • Tile Work • Electrical Work • Plumbing • Heating and Air-Conditioning

Before You Order

1. STUDY THE DESIGNS . . . found in Home Planners current publications. As you review these delightful custom homes, you should keep in mind the total living requirements of your family — both indoors and outdoors. Although we do not make changes in plans, many minor changes can be made prior to the period of construction. If major changes are involved to satisfy your personal requirements, you should consider ordering one set of blueprints and having them redrawn locally. Consultation with your architect is strongly advised when contemplating major changes.

2. HOW TO ORDER BLUEPRINTS . . . After you have chosen the design that satisfies your requirements, or if you have selected one that you wish to study in more detail, simply clip the accompanying order blank and mail with your remittance. However, if it is not convenient for you to send a check or money order, you can use your credit card, or merely indicate C.O.D. shipment. Postman will collect all charges, including postage and C.O.D. fee. C.O.D. shipments are not permitted to Canada or foreign countries. Should time be of essence, as it sometimes is with many of our customers, your telephone order usually can be processed and shipped in the next day's mail. Simply call toll free 1-800-521-6797, (Michigan residents call collect 0-313-477-1854).

3. OUR SERVICE . . . Home Planners makes every effort to process and ship each order for blueprints and books within 48 hours. Because of this, we have deemed it unnecessary to acknowledge receipt of our customers orders. See order coupon for the postage and handling charges for surface mail, air mail or foreign mail.

4. A NOTE REGARDING REVERSE BLUE-PRINTS . . . As a special service to those wishing to build in reverse of the plan as shown, we do include an extra set of reversed blueprints for only $25.00 additional with each order. Even though the lettering and dimensions appear backward on reversed blueprints, they make a handy reference because they show the house just as it's being built in reverse from the standard blueprints — thereby helping you visualize the home better.

5. OUR EXCHANGE POLICY . . . Since blueprints are printed up in specific response to your individual order, we cannot honor requests for refunds. However, the first set of blueprints in any order (or the one set in a single set order) for a given design may be exchanged for a set of another design at a fee of $20.00 plus $3.00 for postage and handling via surface mail; $4.00 via air mail.

TO: **HOME PLANNERS, INC., 23761 RESEARCH DRIVE FARMINGTON HILLS, MICHIGAN 48024**

Please rush me the following:

____ SET(S) BLUEPRINTS FOR DESIGN NO(S). _____ $_____
Single Set, $110.00; Additional Identical Sets in Same Order $25.00 ea.
4 Set Package of Same Design, $165.00 (Save $20.00)
7 Set Package of Same Design, $195.00 (Save $65.00)
(Material Lists and 1 Specification Outline included)
____ SPECIFICATION OUTLINES @ $3.00 EACH . . . . $_____

Michigan Residents add 4% sales tax $_____

FOR POSTAGE AND HANDLING PLEASE CHECK ✔ & REMIT	☐ $3.00 Added to Order for Surface Mail (UPS) – Any Mdse.
	☐ $4.00 Added for Priority Mail of One-Three Sets of Blueprints.
	☐ $6.00 Added for Priority Mail of Four or more Sets of Blueprints.
	☐ For Canadian orders add $2.00 to above applicable rates

$_____

☐ C.O.D. PAY POSTMAN
(C.O.D. Within U.S.A. Only)

TOTAL in U.S.A. funds $_____

PLEASE PRINT
Name _____
Street _____
City _____ State _____ Zip _____

CREDIT CARD ORDERS ONLY: Fill in the boxes below

Prices subject to change without notice

Credit Card No. [☐☐☐☐☐☐☐☐☐☐☐☐☐☐☐]   Expiration Date Month/Year [☐☐☐☐]

CHECK ONE: ☐ VISA   ☐ MasterCard

Order Form Key 108BP

Your Signature _____

BLUEPRINT ORDERS SHIPPED WITHIN 48 HOURS OF RECEIPT!

TO: **HOME PLANNERS, INC., 23761 RESEARCH DRIVE FARMINGTON HILLS, MICHIGAN 48024**

Please rush me the following:

____ SET(S) BLUEPRINTS FOR DESIGN NO(S). _____ $_____
Single Set, $110.00; Additional Identical Sets in Same Order $25.00 ea.
4 Set Package of Same Design, $165.00 (Save $20.00)
7 Set Package of Same Design, $195.00 (Save $65.00)
(Material Lists and 1 Specification Outline included)
____ SPECIFICATION OUTLINES @ $3.00 EACH . . . . $_____

Michigan Residents add 4% sales tax $_____

FOR POSTAGE AND HANDLING PLEASE CHECK ✔ & REMIT	☐ $3.00 Added to Order for Surface Mail (UPS) – Any Mdse.
	☐ $4.00 Added for Priority Mail of One-Three Sets of Blueprints.
	☐ $6.00 Added for Priority Mail of Four or more Sets of Blueprints.
	☐ For Canadian orders add $2.00 to above applicable rates

$_____

☐ C.O.D. PAY POSTMAN
(C.O.D. Within U.S.A. Only)

TOTAL in U.S.A. funds $_____

PLEASE PRINT
Name _____
Street _____
City _____ State _____ Zip _____

CREDIT CARD ORDERS ONLY: Fill in the boxes below

Prices subject to change without notice

Credit Card No. [☐☐☐☐☐☐☐☐☐☐☐☐☐☐☐]   Expiration Date Month/Year [☐☐☐☐]

CHECK ONE: ☐ VISA   ☐ MasterCard

Order Form Key 108BP

Your Signature _____

How many sets of blueprints should be ordered?

This question is often asked. The answer can range anywhere from 1 to 7 sets, depending upon circumstances. For instance, a single set of blueprints of your favorite design is sufficient to study the house in greater detail. On the other hand, if you are planning to get cost estimates, or if you are planning to build, you may need as many as seven sets of blueprints. Because the first set of blueprints in each order is $110.00, and because additional sets of the same design in each order are only $25.00 each (and with package sets even more economical), you save considerably by ordering your total requirements now. To help you determine the exact number of sets, please refer to the handy check list.

How Many Blueprints Do You Need?

__OWNER'S SET

__BUILDER (Usually requires at least 3 sets: 1 as legal document; 1 for inspection; and at least 1 for tradesmen — usually more.)

__BUILDING PERMIT (Sometimes 2 sets are required.)

__MORTGAGE SOURCE (Usually 1 set for a conventional mortgage; 3 sets for F.H.A. or V.A. type mortgages.)

__SUBDIVISION COMMITTEE (If any.)

__TOTAL NO. SETS REQUIRED

Blueprint Ordering Hotline –

Phone toll free: 1-800-521-6797.
Orders received by 11 a.m. (Detroit time) will be processed the same day and shipped to you the following day. Use of this line restricted to blueprint ordering only. Michigan residents simply call collect 0-313-477-1854.

Kindly Note: When ordering by phone, please state Order Form Key No. located in box at lower left corner of blueprint order form.

In Canada Mail To:
Home Planners, Inc., 20 Cedar St. North
Kitchener, Ontario N2H 2W8
Phone: (519) 743-4169

A Potpourri of Designs
Offering Varied Styles for All Budgets

DINING RM.
10⁰x11⁶

COUNTRY KITCHEN
21⁰x13⁶-10⁶

RANGE

SNACKS.

REF'G

DESK   CHINA/PANTRY

BRM CL   DN   PDR RM

CL

LIVING RM.
13⁰x15⁶   FOYER   CL   STUDY
11⁰x9¹⁰

UP

PORCH

TERRACE

32'-0"

30'-0"

ROOF

BATH   BATH

LINEN   DN

CL   CL

BEDROOM
10⁸x13⁴   MASTER BEDROOM
12⁴x13⁴

CL   CL

ACCESS TO STORAGE AREA   STORAGE AREA

ROOF

Design 82852 919 Sq. Ft. - First Floor; 535 Sq. Ft. - Second Floor; 24,450 Cu. Ft.

● This charming house will make an excellent first home or retirement retreat. Inside this compact frame is a very livable plan. One of the most outstanding features is the spacious country kitchen. Notice the work island with snack bar and range, desk, and china/pantry storage. Access to the rear terrace can be obtained through the kitchen and dining room doors. Adjacent to the dining room is a large living room. Take note of the fireplace that will bring many hours of pleasure on cold winter evenings. Also, a nice sized study and powder room are on the first floor. Two full baths and two bedrooms are on the second floor of this quaint one-and-a-half story design.

Design 82847
1,874 Sq. Ft. - Main Level
1,131 Sq. Ft. - Lower Level; 44,305 Cu. Ft.

● This is an exquisitely styled Tudor, hillside design, ready to serve its happy occupants for many years. The contrasting use of material surely makes the exterior eye-catching.

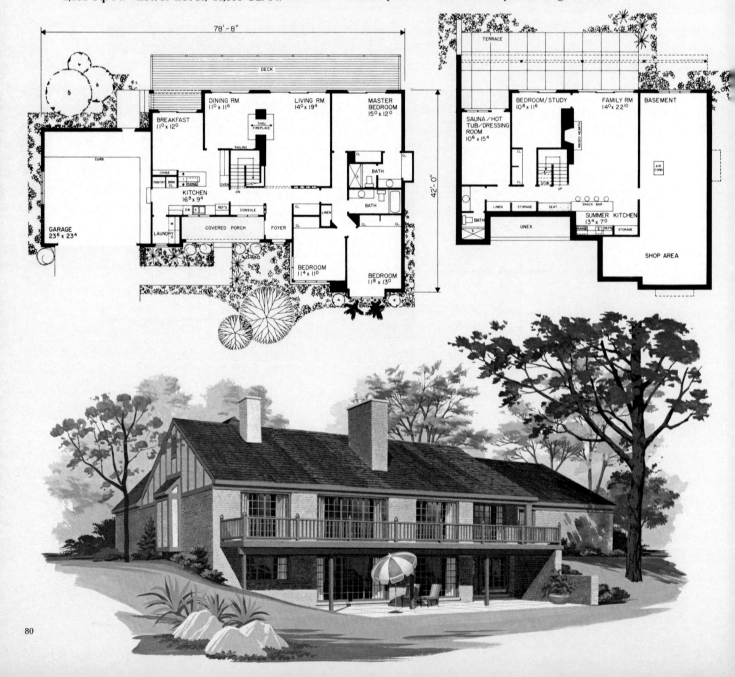

Design 82846
2,341 Sq. Ft. - Main Level; 1,380 Sq. Ft. - Lower Level; 51,290 Cu. Ft.

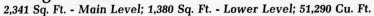

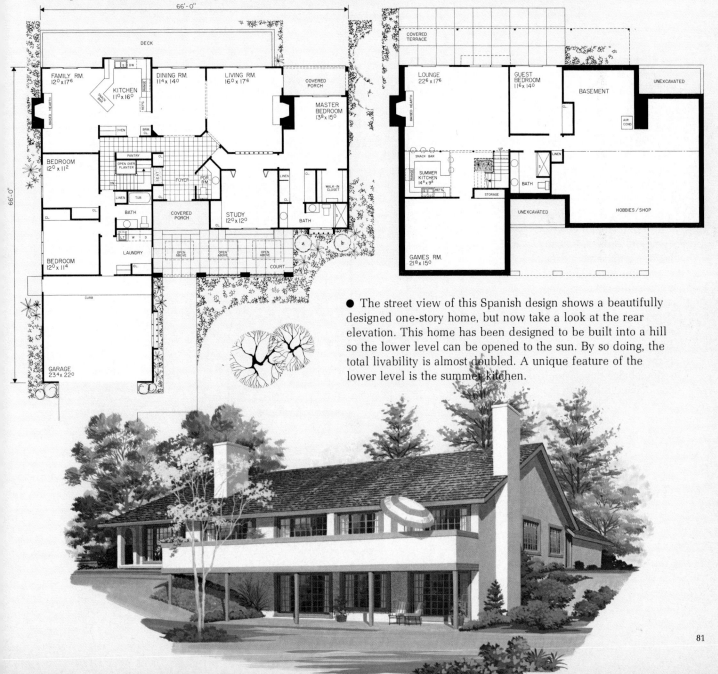

● The street view of this Spanish design shows a beautifully designed one-story home, but now take a look at the rear elevation. This home has been designed to be built into a hill so the lower level can be opened to the sun. By so doing, the total livability is almost doubled. A unique feature of the lower level is the summer kitchen.

Design 82730
2,490 Sq. Ft.; 50,340 Cu. Ft.

● Here is a basic one-story home that is really loaded with livability on the first floor and has a bonus of an extra 1,086 sq. ft. of planned livability on a lower level. What makes this so livable is that the first floor, adjacent to the stairs leading below, is open and forms a balcony looking down into a dramatic planting area. The first floor traffic patterns flow around this impressive and distinctive feature. In addition to the gathering room, study and family room, there is the lounge and activity room. Notice the second balcony open to the activity room below. The master bedroom is outstanding with two baths and two walk-in closets. The attached three-car garage has a bulk storage area and is accessible through the service area.

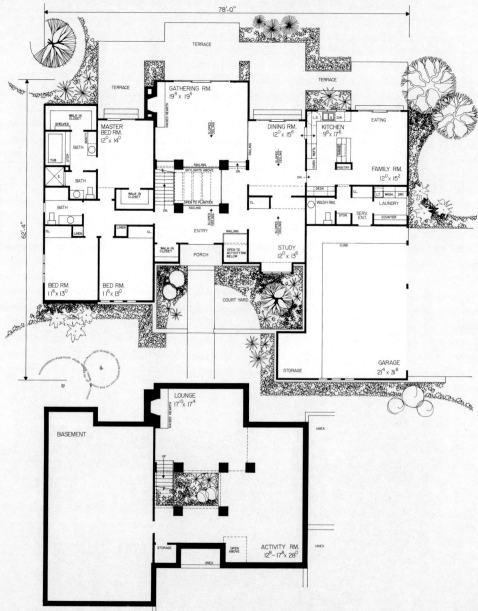

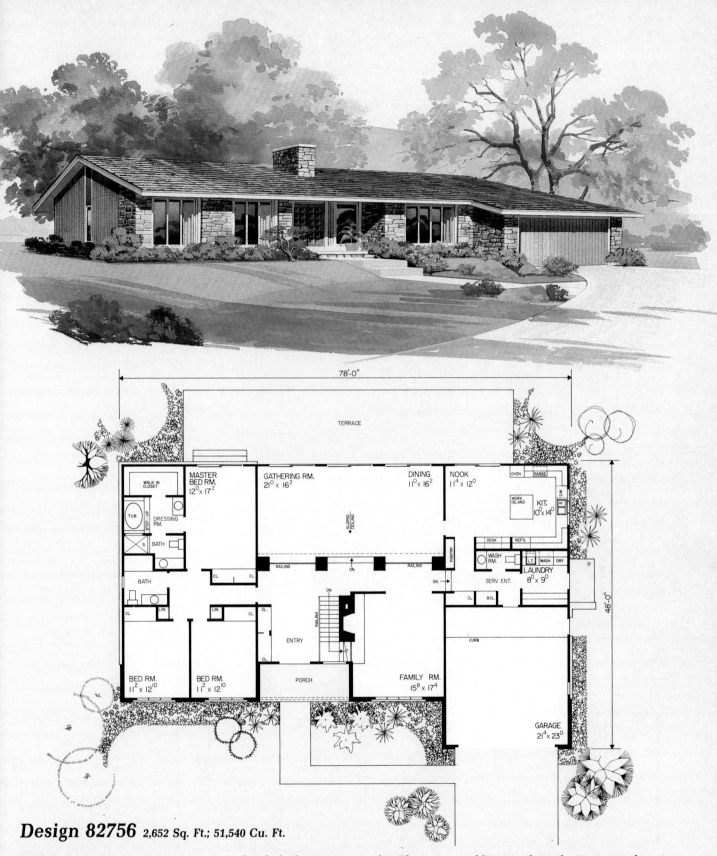

Labels within the floor plan:

78'-0"

TERRACE

WALK-IN CLOSET

MASTER BED RM.
12⁰ x 17²

GATHERING RM.
21⁰ x 16²

DINING
11⁰ x 16²

NOOK
11⁴ x 12⁰

OVEN | RANGE

TUB

STEP-UP

DRESSING RM.

BATH

S.

SLOPED CEILING

WORK ISLAND

KIT.
10⁰ x 14⁰

DESK | REFG.

BATH

CL. | CL.

RAILING

DN.

RAILING

PANTRY

WASH RM.

LT. | WASH | DRY

LAUNDRY
8⁰ x 9⁰

P.

CL. | LIN.

LIN. | CL. | CL.

CL.

DN.

SERV. ENT.

CL. | B.CL.

DN.

ENTRY

RAILING

BED RM.
11² x 12¹⁰

BED RM.
11² x 12¹⁰

PORCH

FAMILY RM.
15⁸ x 17⁴

CURB

48'-0"

GARAGE
21⁴ x 23⁰

Design 82756   2,652 Sq. Ft.; 51,540 Cu. Ft.

● This one-story contemporary is bound to serve your family well. It will assure the best in contemporary living with its many fine features. Notice the bath with tub and stall shower, dressing room and walk-in closet featured with the master bedroom. Two more family bedrooms are nearby. The sunken gathering/dining room is highlighted by the sloped ceiling and sliding glass doors to the large rear terrace. This formal area is a full 32' x 16'. Imagine the great furniture placement that can be done in this area. In addition to the gathering room, there is an informal family room with fireplace. You will enjoy the efficient kitchen and get much use out of the work island, pantry and built-in desk. Note the service entrance with bath and laundry.

Design 82149

988 Sq. Ft. - First Floor
952 Sq. Ft. - Second Floor; 30,438 Cu. Ft.

● Any one of these exteriors can be built with the floor plan below. If you like the traditional version to the left, order blueprints for 82149; if you prefer the Farmhouse adaptation below, order 82150; should your choice be for the Tudor variation at the bottom, order 82151. Whatever your selection, you'll appreciate your new home.

Design 82150

991 Sq. Ft. - First Floor
952 Sq. Ft. - Second Floor; 27,850 Cu. Ft.

● In each of these designs the attached two-car garage adds to the appeal as its roof continues to provide a covered porch for the front doors. A professional builder could hardly do better than to find a place for these charming houses in his subdivision. The basically rectangular shape of the main house will mean economical construction.

Design 82151

991 Sq. Ft. - First Floor
952 Sq. Ft. - Second Floor; 28,964 Cu. Ft.

● The blueprints you order will show details for building either the four or the five bedroom version. Which will serve your family best? In addition to the two baths of the second floor, there is an extra powder room. Further, there is a laundry, separate dining room, family room, U-shaped kitchen and basement. A great plan for the modest budget.

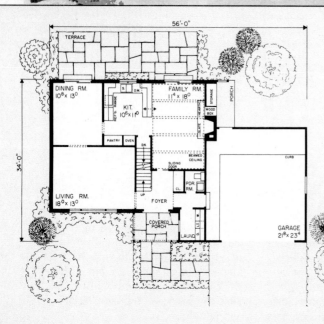

OPTIONAL 4 BEDROOM PLAN

Design 82750
1,209 Sq. Ft. - First Floor
965 Sq. Ft. - Second Floor; 32,025 Cu. Ft.

● These impressive two-story homes will catch the eye of the on-lookers. The extended one-story wings at each end of the house add appeal to the exterior. The covered porch also is a charming feature. No matter which of these delightful exteriors that you choose, you will receive a home to serve your family for a lifetime.

Design 82751
1,202 Sq. Ft. - First Floor
964 Sq. Ft. - Second Floor; 33,830 Cu. Ft.

● Now take a walk through the efficient floor plan. The living/dining room is L-shaped with the dining room being convenient to the kitchen. The kitchen has a pass-thru to the breakfast nook plus many built-ins to help ease kitchen duties. The nook, along with the family room, has sliding glass doors to the terrace.

Design 82752
1,209 Sq. Ft. - First Floor
960 Sq. Ft. - Second Floor; 34,725 Cu. Ft.

● Also on the first floor is a powder room and laundry. The second floor houses the three family bedrooms, bath and the master bedroom suite with all the extras. Order Design 82750 for the Mansard roofed exterior; Design 82751 for the Colonial with the Gambrel roof and for the Farmhouse type design, order 82752.

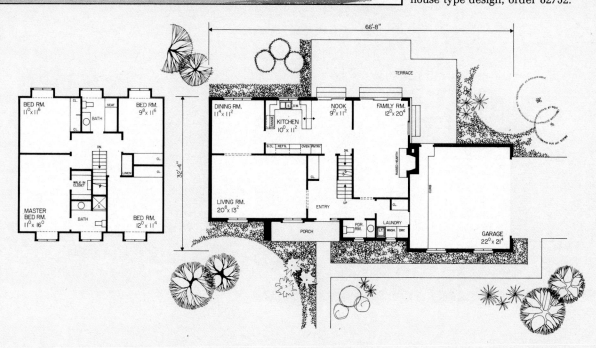

Design 82779 3,225 Sq. Ft.; 70,715 Cu. Ft.

● This French design is surely impressive. The exterior appearance will brighten any area with its French roof, paned-glass windows, masonry brick privacy wall and double front doors. The inside is just as appealing. Note the unique placement of rooms and features. Enter this home into the entry hall. It is large and leads to each of the areas in this plan. To the left, the formal dining room is outstanding. While serving a formal dinner one can enter by way of the butler's pantry (notice it's size and that it has a sink). To the right of the entry is a sizable parlor and beyond that is the three bedroom sleeping area. The gathering room with fireplace, sliding glass doors and adjacent study is in the back of the plan. The work center is also outstanding. There is the U-shaped kitchen, island range, snack bar, breakfast nook, pantry plus wash room and large laundry near service entrance.

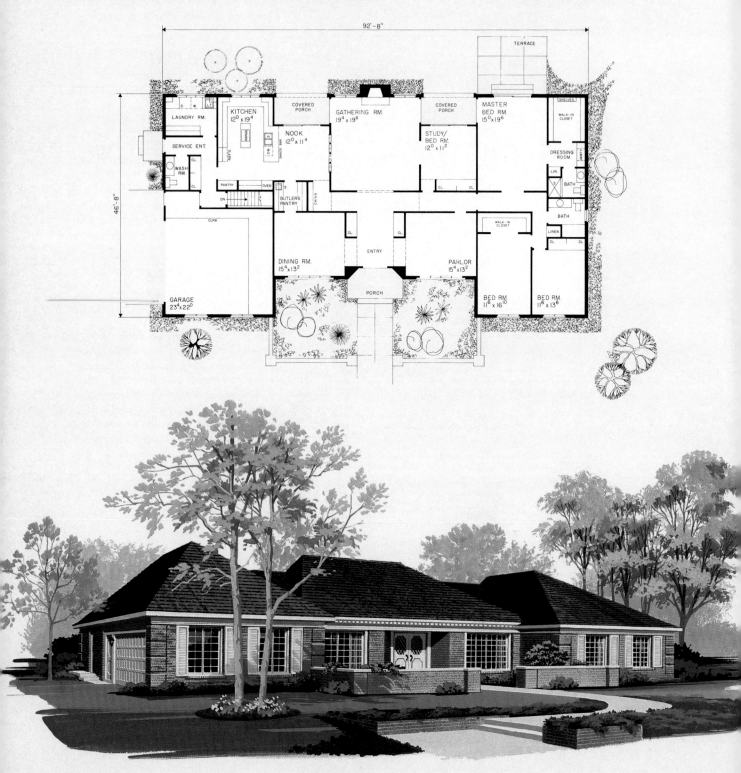

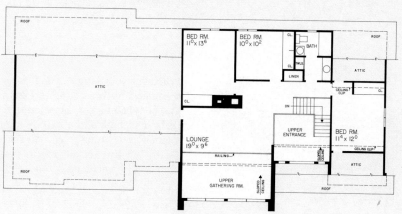

BED RM. 11⁰ x 13⁶
BED RM. 10⁰ x 10²
BATH
CL.
TWLS.
LINEN
ATTIC
CL.
ROOF
ROOF
ATTIC
CEILING? CLIP
CL.
CL.
LOUNGE 19⁰ x 9⁶
DN
UPPER ENTRANCE
BED RM. 11⁴ x 12⁰
CEILING CLIP
RAILING
SLOPED CEILING
ATTIC
ROOF
UPPER GATHERING RM.
SLOPED CEILING
ROOF

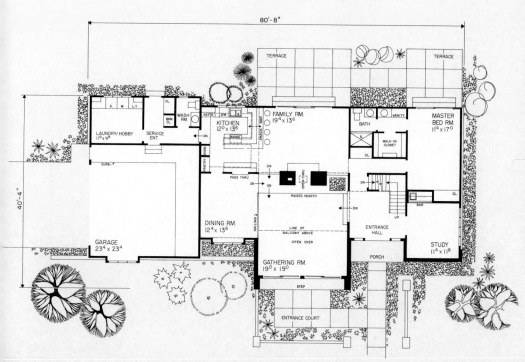

80'- 8"

TERRACE
TERRACE

LAUNDRY/HOBBY 11⁰ x 9⁸
SERVICE ENT.
D. W. L. T.
CL.
BRM. CL.
WASH RM.
REFR.
D.W.
KITCHEN
FAMILY RM. 19⁴ x 13⁶
BATH
VANITY
MASTER BED RM. 11⁴ x 17⁰

RANGE
SNACK BAR
WALK-IN CLOSET
CL.

40'- 4"

PANTRY
PASS THRU
DN
DN
DN
OPEN THRU
DN
BAR

GARAGE 23⁴ x 23⁴
CURB
DINING RM. 12⁴ x 13⁶
RAISED HEARTH
DN
UP
ENTRANCE HALL
STUDY 11⁴ x 11⁸

LINE OF BALCONY ABOVE
OPEN OVER
RAILING
GATHERING RM. 19⁰ x 19⁰
PORCH

STEP

ENTRANCE COURT

Design 82782

2,060 Sq. Ft. - First Floor
897 Sq. Ft. - Second Floor
47,750 Cu. Ft.

● What makes this such a distinctive four bedroom design? Let's list some of the features. This plan includes great formal and informal living for the family at home or when entertaining guests. The formal gathering room and informal family room share a dramatic raised-hearth fireplace. Other features of the sunken gathering room include: high, sloped ceilings, built-in planter and sliding glass doors to the front entrance court. The kitchen has a snack bar, many built-ins, a pass-thru to dining room and easy access to the large laundry/wash room. The master bedroom suite is located on the main level for added privacy and convenience. There's even a study with a built-in bar. The upper level has three more bedrooms, a bath and a lounge looking down into the gathering room.

● If you can't make up your mind as to which of the delightful, traditional exteriors you like best on this page, you need not decide now. The blueprints you receive show details for the construction of all three front exteriors.

However, before you order, decide whether you wish your next home to have a basement or not. If you prefer the basement plan order Design 82153, the left plan below. Should your preference be for a non-basement plan you should order blueprints for Design 82154, right below.

Whatever your choice, you'll forever love the charm of its exterior and the comfort and convenience of the interior. The three bedrooms, bath and a half, living room and kitchen and dining room will serve your family ideally. Rectangular in shape, this home will be economical to build.

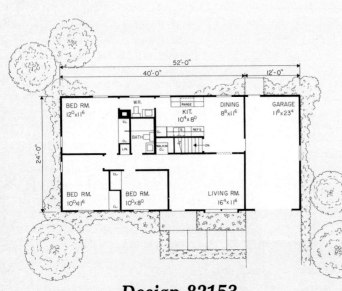

Design 82153
960 Sq. Ft.; 18,432 Cu. Ft.

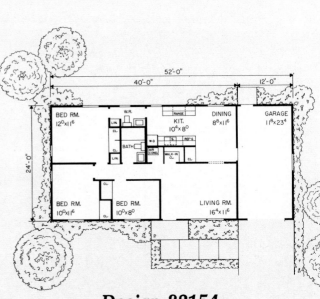

Design 82154
960 Sq. Ft.; 10,675 Cu. Ft.

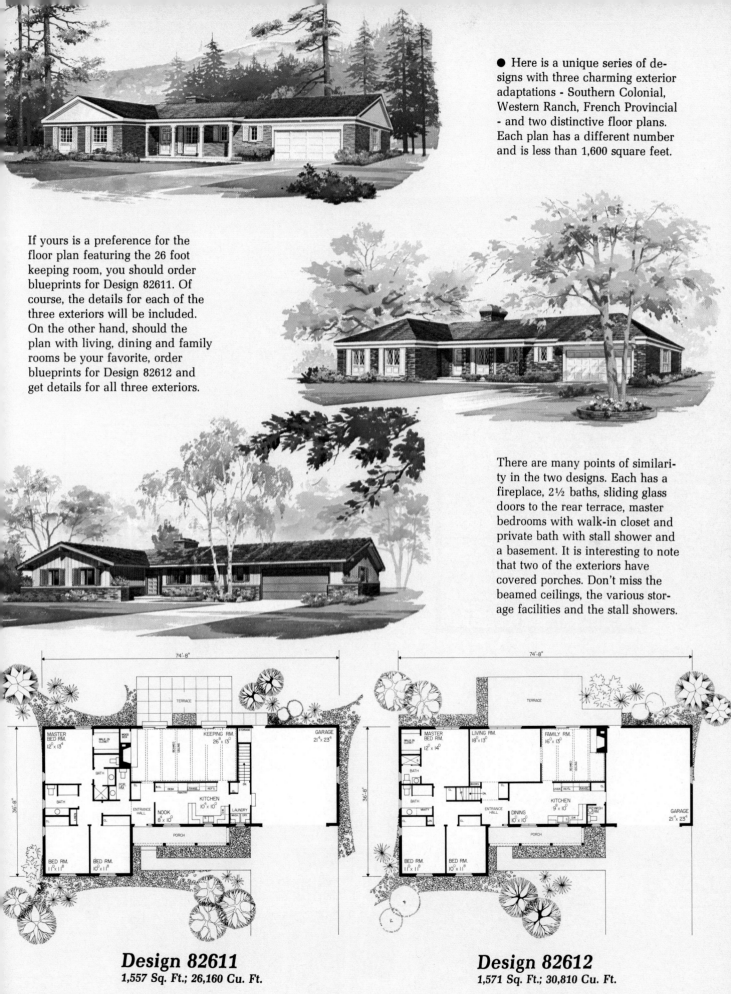

● Here is a unique series of designs with three charming exterior adaptations - Southern Colonial, Western Ranch, French Provincial - and two distinctive floor plans. Each plan has a different number and is less than 1,600 square feet.

If yours is a preference for the floor plan featuring the 26 foot keeping room, you should order blueprints for Design 82611. Of course, the details for each of the three exteriors will be included. On the other hand, should the plan with living, dining and family rooms be your favorite, order blueprints for Design 82612 and get details for all three exteriors.

There are many points of similarity in the two designs. Each has a fireplace, 2½ baths, sliding glass doors to the rear terrace, master bedrooms with walk-in closet and private bath with stall shower and a basement. It is interesting to note that two of the exteriors have covered porches. Don't miss the beamed ceilings, the various storage facilities and the stall showers.

Design 82611
1,557 Sq. Ft.; 26,160 Cu. Ft.

Design 82612
1,571 Sq. Ft.; 30,810 Cu. Ft.

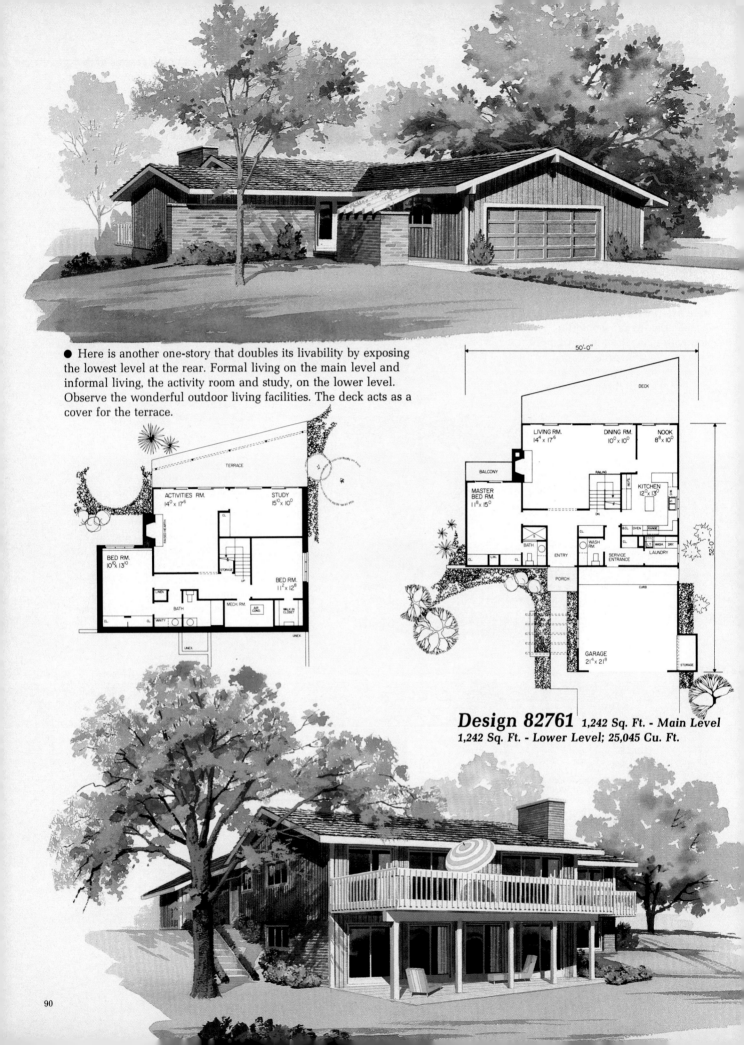

● Here is another one-story that doubles its livability by exposing the lowest level at the rear. Formal living on the main level and informal living, the activity room and study, on the lower level. Observe the wonderful outdoor living facilities. The deck acts as a cover for the terrace.

TERRACE

ACTIVITIES RM.
14⁰ x 17⁶

STUDY
15¹⁰ x 10⁰

BED RM.
10¹⁰ x 13¹⁰

CL.

STORAGE

UP

BED RM.
11² x 12⁸

LINEN

BATH

VANITY

MECH. RM.

AIR COND.

WALK IN CLOSET

CL. CL.

UNEX.

UNEX.

50'-0"

DECK

LIVING RM.
14⁴ x 17⁶

DINING RM.
10⁰ x 10⁰

NOOK
8⁸ x 10⁰

BALCONY

RAILING

REFG.

KITCHEN
12⁰ x 13⁰

MASTER
BED RM.
11⁸ x 15⁰

DN

B.C. OVEN RANGE

DW

BATH

CL.

ENTRY

WASH RM.

SERVICE ENTRANCE

CL.

LT. WASH DRY

LAUNDRY

CL. LIN. CL.

PORCH

CURB

52'-0"

GARAGE
21⁴ x 21⁸

STORAGE

Design 82761 1,242 Sq. Ft. - Main Level
1,242 Sq. Ft. - Lower Level; 25,045 Cu. Ft.

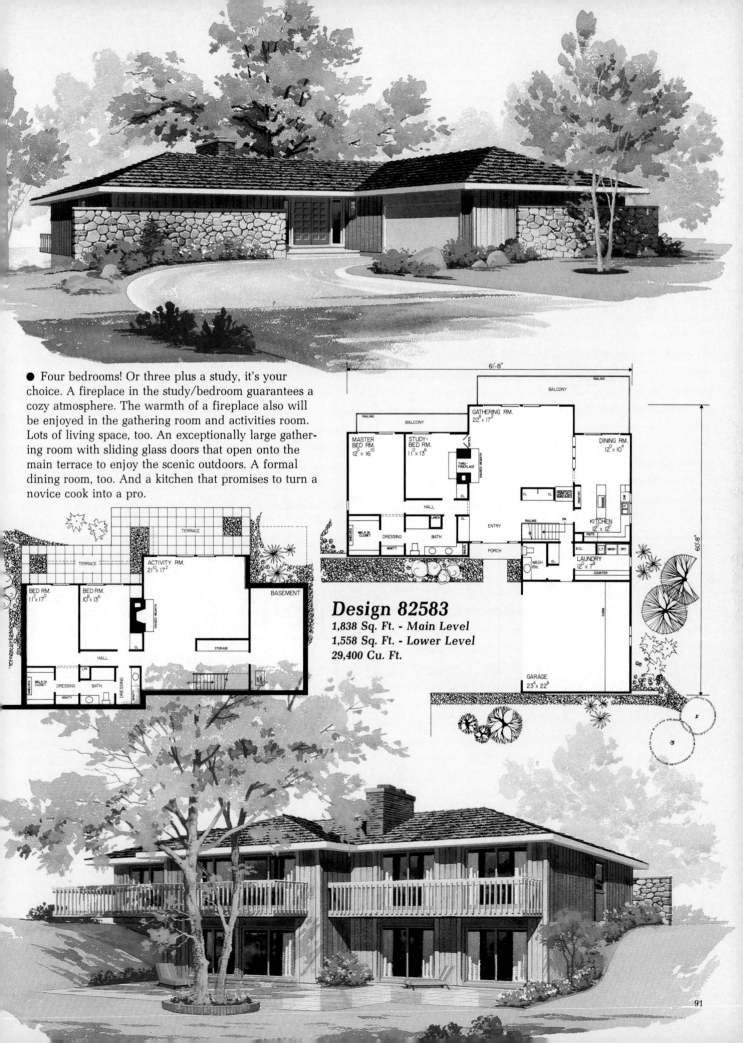

● Four bedrooms! Or three plus a study, it's your choice. A fireplace in the study/bedroom guarantees a cozy atmosphere. The warmth of a fireplace also will be enjoyed in the gathering room and activities room. Lots of living space, too. An exceptionally large gathering room with sliding glass doors that open onto the main terrace to enjoy the scenic outdoors. A formal dining room, too. And a kitchen that promises to turn a novice cook into a pro.

Design 82583
1,838 Sq. Ft. - Main Level
1,558 Sq. Ft. - Lower Level
29,400 Cu. Ft.

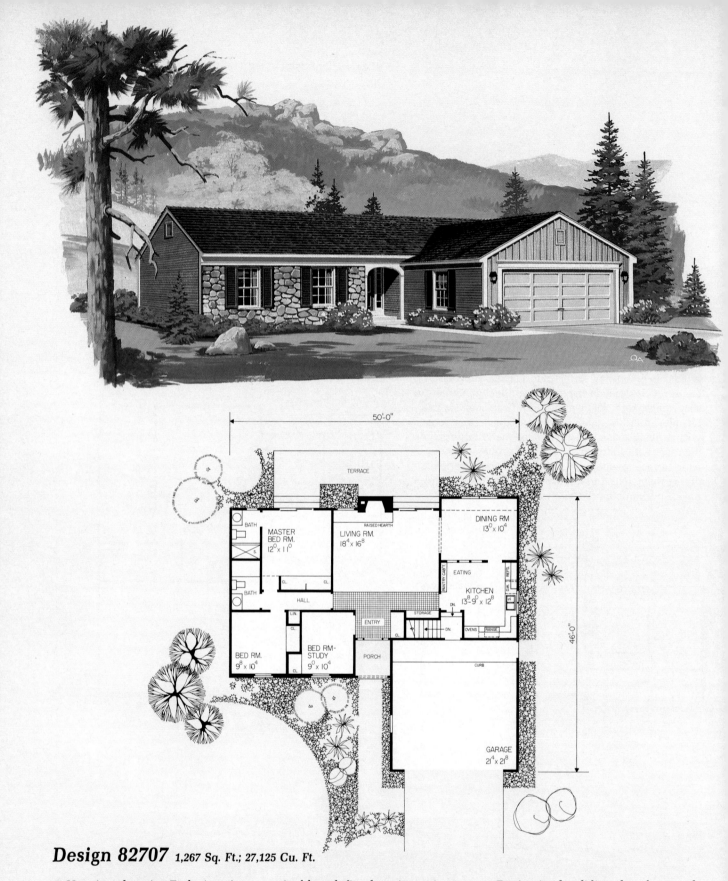

Design 82707 *1,267 Sq. Ft.; 27,125 Cu. Ft.*

● Here is a charming Early American adaptation that will serve as a picturesque and practical retirement home. This plan is also perfect for those with a small family in search of an efficient, economically built home. The centrally located living area, highlighted by the raised hearth fireplace, is spacious. The kitchen features eating space and easy access to the garage and basement. Adjacent to the kitchen, the dining room has an excellent view of the rear yard. The bedroom wing offers three bedrooms and two full baths.

Don't miss the sliding glass doors to the terrace from the living room and the master bedroom. Storage units are plentiful including a pantry cabinet in the eating area of the kitchen. There is a good-sized basement for recreation and hobby pursuits.

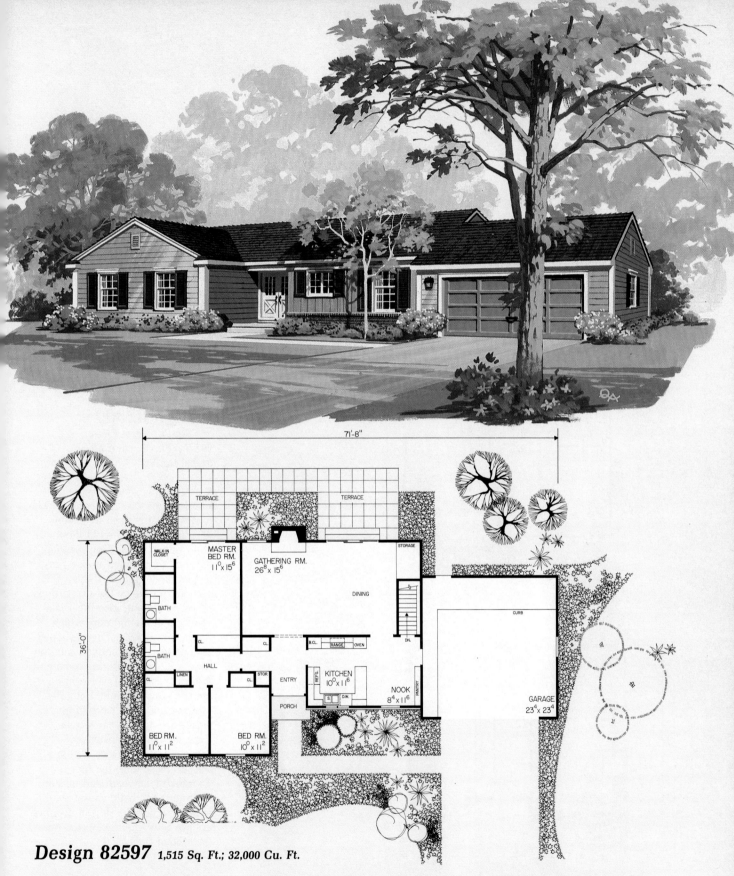

TERRACE

TERRACE

STORAGE

WALK-IN CLOSET

MASTER BED RM.
11⁰ x 15⁶

GATHERING RM.
26⁸ x 15⁶

DINING

BATH

CL.

CL.

B.CL.

RANGE OVEN

DN.

CURB

BATH

HALL

CL.

LINEN

CL.

STOR.

ENTRY

KITCHEN
10⁰ x 11⁶

REFG.

NOOK
8⁴ x 11⁶

PANTRY

GARAGE
23⁴ x 23⁴

CL.

PORCH

S D.W.

BED RM.
11⁰ x 11²

BED RM.
10⁰ x 11²

71'-8"

36'-0"

Design 82597 1,515 Sq. Ft.; 32,000 Cu. Ft.

● Whether it be a starter house you are after, or one in which to spend your retirement years, this pleasing frame home will provide a full measure of pride of ownership. The contrast of vertical and horizontal lines, the double front doors and the coach lamp post at the garage create an inviting exterior. Efficiently planned, the floor plan functions in an orderly manner. The 26 foot gathering room has a delightful view of the rear yard and will take care of those formal dining occasions. There are two full baths serving the three bedrooms. Additional features include: plenty of storage facilities, two sets of glass doors to the terraces, a fireplace in the gathering room, a basement and an attached two-car garage to act as a buffer against the wind.

BEDROOM
15⁰ x 12⁰

BATH

SHLVS.
S.
WALK-IN
CLOSET

LINEN
BATH

VANITY

HALL

DN

NURSERY/
STUDY
8⁴ x 9⁴

MASTER
BEDROOM
11⁰ x 16⁸

BEDROOM
12⁰ x 12⁴

CL.

TERRACE

58'-0"

28'-8"

DINING RM.
10⁰ + BAY x 11⁸

KIT.
9⁶ x 11⁸

D.W.
S

RANGE

BRKFST. RM.
8⁰ x 10⁶

CHINA

W.R.

MUD. RM.

REF'G.

BRM
CL.
W.
D.

CURB

PANTRY

CL.

DN

FOYER

UP

FAMILY RM.
11⁰ x 13¹⁰+BAY

GARAGE
21⁴ x 22⁸

LIVING RM.
14⁰ x 15⁴

PORCH

Design 82800

999 Sq. Ft. - First Floor
997 Sq. Ft. - Second Floor
31,390 Cu. Ft.

● This Tudor design has many
fine features to make its mark. The
exterior is enhanced by a front
and side bay window in the family
and dining rooms. Along with an
outstanding exterior, it also contains a modern and efficient floor
plan within its modest proportions.
Flanking the entrance foyer is a
comfortable living room which
houses a fireplace. The U-shaped
kitchen is conveniently located between the formal dining room and
the breakfast room which has a
built-in china cabinet. Both of
these eating areas have sliding
glass doors to the rear terrace.
Even though this design has a
basement, the laundry facilities
are still located on the first floor.
Two bedrooms, bath and master
bedroom with bath, vanity, walk-
in closet and adjoining study/nurs-
ery are conveniently located on
the second floor.

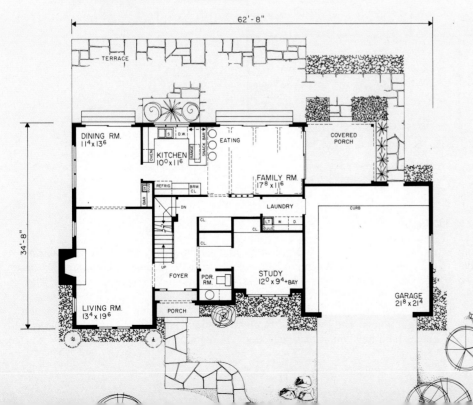

Design 82854

1,261 Sq. Ft. - First Floor
950 Sq. Ft. - Second Floor
36,820 Cu. Ft.

● The flair of old England has been captured in this outstanding one-and-a-half story design. Interior livability will efficiently serve the various needs of all family members. The first floor offers both formal and informal areas, along with the work centers. Note some of the various features which include a wet-bar in the dining room, the kitchen's snack bar, first floor laundry and rear covered porch to mention a few. Accommodations for sleeping will be found on the second floor. There are two family bedrooms and the master bedroom suite. Don't miss the uniqueness of the lounge/nursery area which is attached to the master bedroom.

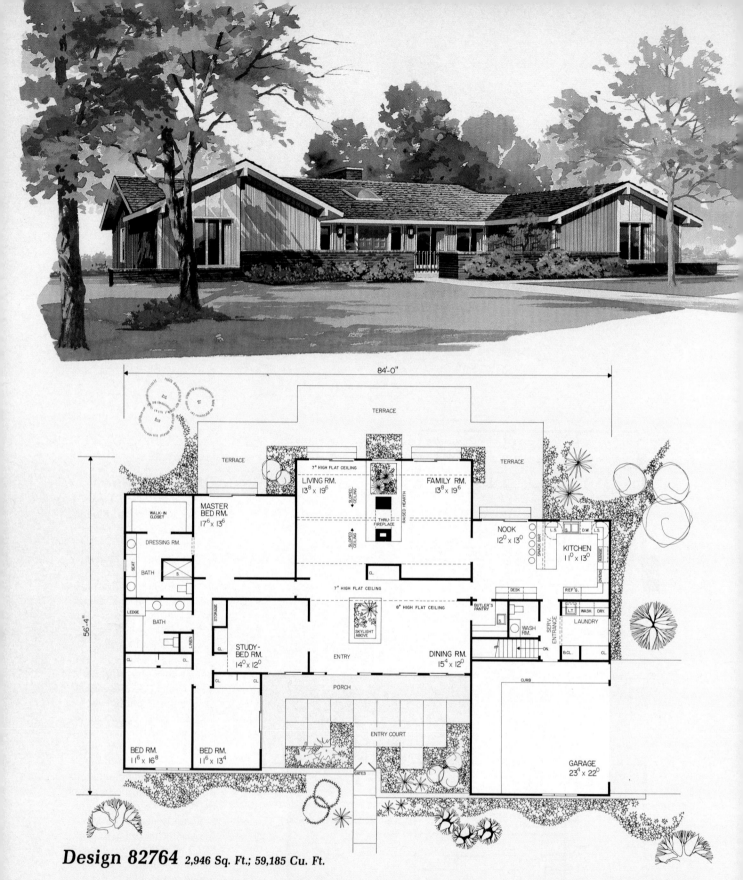

Design 82764 *2,946 Sq. Ft.; 59,185 Cu. Ft.*

● If uniqueness is what you're looking for in your new home, then this three (optional four) bedroom design will be ideal. Notice the large, gated-in entry court, vertical paned windows and contrasting exterior materials. All of these features compose an attractive design suitable for any location. Within but a second after entering this home one will be confronted with features galore. The entry/dining area has a focal point of a built-in planter with a skylight above. The living and family rooms both have an attractive sloped ceiling. They share a raised hearth, thru-fireplace and both have access to the large wrap-around terrace. The kitchen-nook area also has access to the terrace and has the features of a snack bar, built-in desk and large butler's pantry.

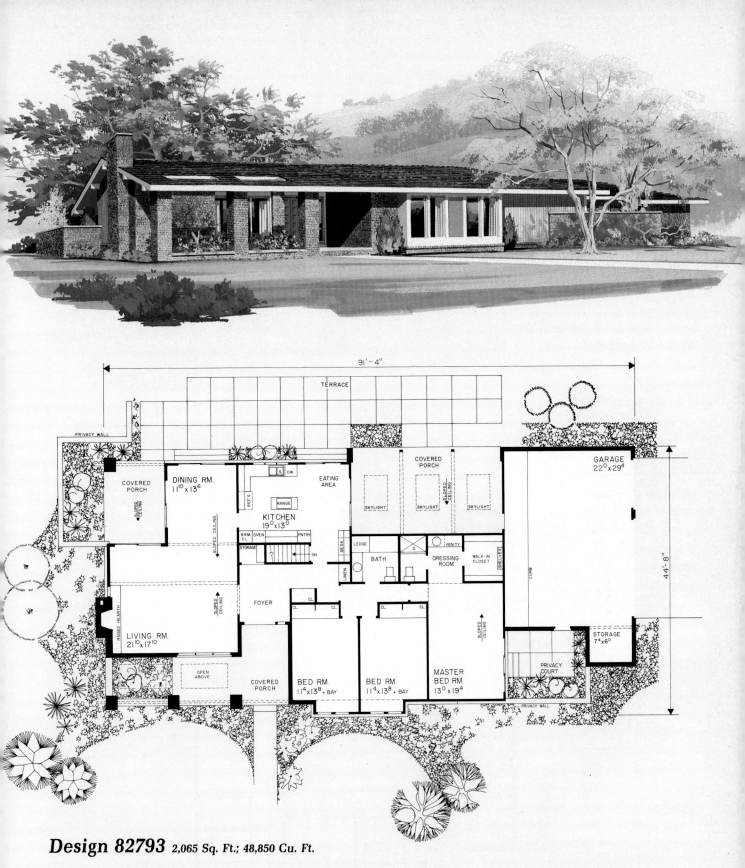

Design 82793 *2,065 Sq. Ft.; 48,850 Cu. Ft.*

● Privacy will be enjoyed in this home both inside and out. The indoor-outdoor living relationships offered in this plan are outstanding. A covered porch at the entrance. A privacy court off the master bedroom divided from the front yard with a privacy wall. A covered porch serving both the living and dining rooms through sliding glass doors. Also utilizing a privacy wall. Another covered porch off the kitchen eating area. This one is the largest and has skylights above. Also a large rear terrace. The kitchen is efficient with eating space available, an island range and built-in desk. Storage space is abundant. Note storage area in the garage and its overall size. Three front bedrooms. Raised hearth fireplace in the living room.

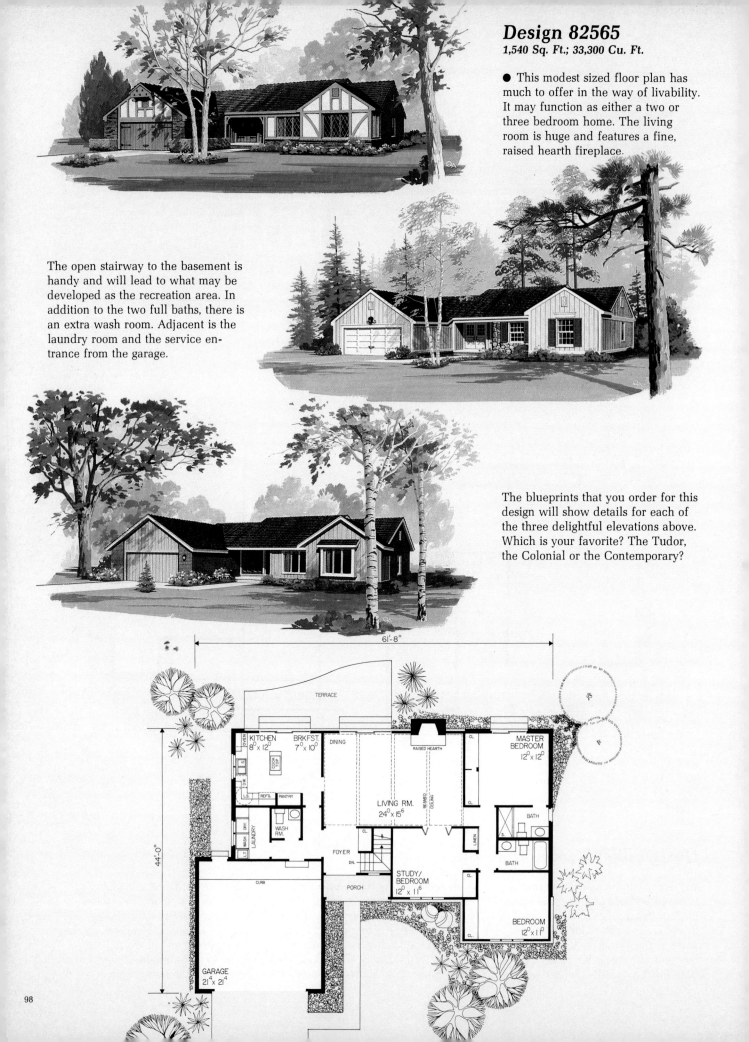

Design 82565
1,540 Sq. Ft.; 33,300 Cu. Ft.

● This modest sized floor plan has much to offer in the way of livability. It may function as either a two or three bedroom home. The living room is huge and features a fine, raised hearth fireplace.

The open stairway to the basement is handy and will lead to what may be developed as the recreation area. In addition to the two full baths, there is an extra wash room. Adjacent is the laundry room and the service entrance from the garage.

The blueprints that you order for this design will show details for each of the three delightful elevations above. Which is your favorite? The Tudor, the Colonial or the Contemporary?

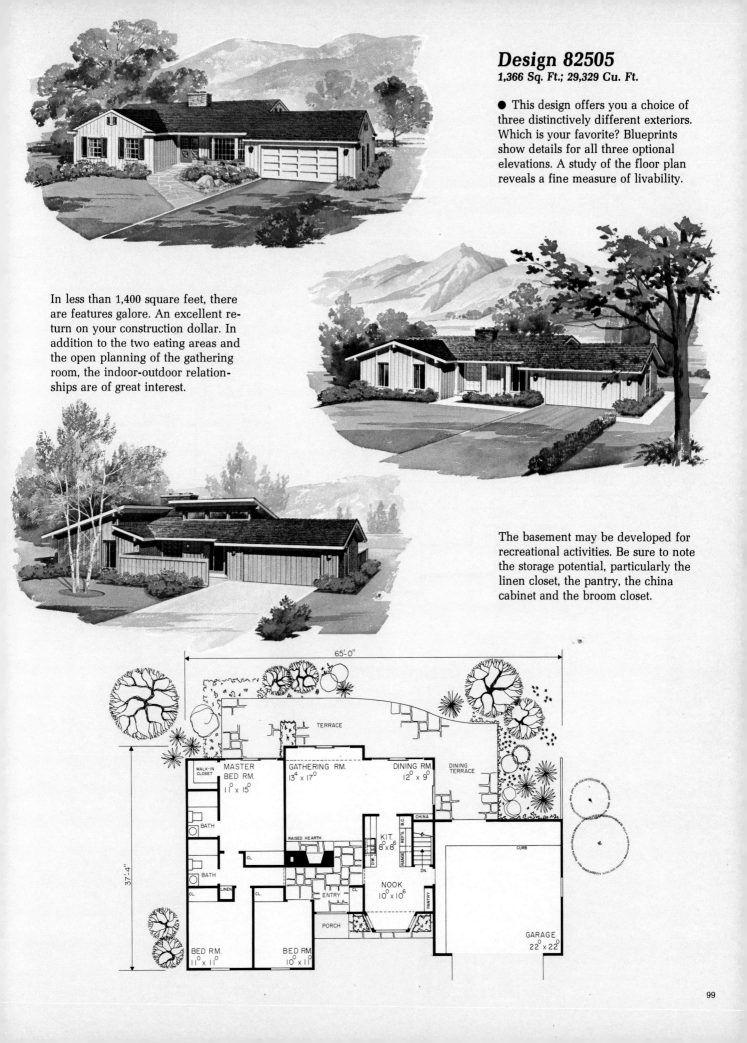

Design 82505
1,366 Sq. Ft.; 29,329 Cu. Ft.

● This design offers you a choice of three distinctively different exteriors. Which is your favorite? Blueprints show details for all three optional elevations. A study of the floor plan reveals a fine measure of livability.

In less than 1,400 square feet, there are features galore. An excellent return on your construction dollar. In addition to the two eating areas and the open planning of the gathering room, the indoor-outdoor relationships are of great interest.

The basement may be developed for recreational activities. Be sure to note the storage potential, particularly the linen closet, the pantry, the china cabinet and the broom closet.

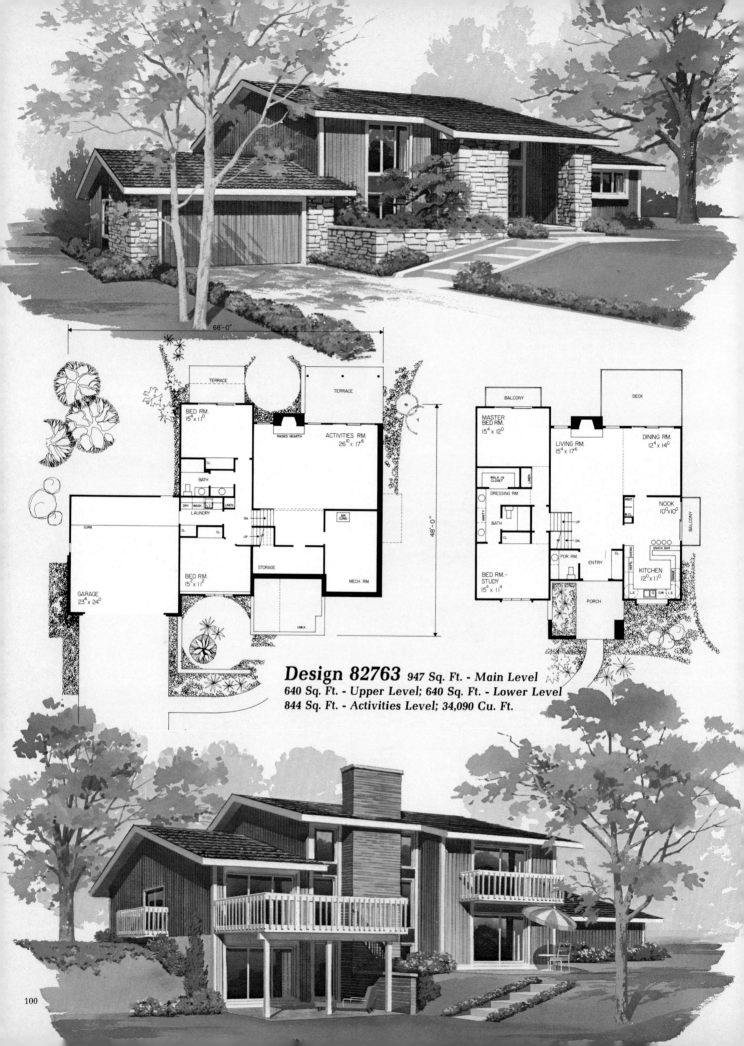

68'-0"

48'-0"

TERRACE

TERRACE

BED RM.
15⁴ x 11⁰

ACTIVITIES RM.
26¹⁰ x 17⁶

RAISED HEARTH

CL.

BATH

DRY. WASH. LINEN

LAUNDRY

DN.

AIR
COND.

CURB

CL.

UP

CL.

GARAGE
23⁴ x 24⁰

BED RM.
15⁴ x 11²

STORAGE

MECH. RM.

UNEX.

BALCONY

DECK

MASTER
BED RM.
15⁴ x 12⁰

LIVING RM.
15⁴ x 17⁶

DINING RM.
12⁴ x 14⁰

WALK-IN
CLOSET

LINEN

PLANT.

DRESSING RM.

NOOK
10⁰ x 10⁰

BALCONY

VANITY

BATH

CL.

UP

B.CL.

SNACK BAR

DN.

PDR. RM.

ENTRY

CL.

KITCHEN
12⁰ x 11⁰

BED RM.-
STUDY
15⁴ x 11⁴

PORCH

L.S.

S

D.W.

L.S.

Design 82763 947 Sq. Ft. - Main Level
640 Sq. Ft. - Upper Level; 640 Sq. Ft. - Lower Level
844 Sq. Ft. - Activities Level; 34,090 Cu. Ft.

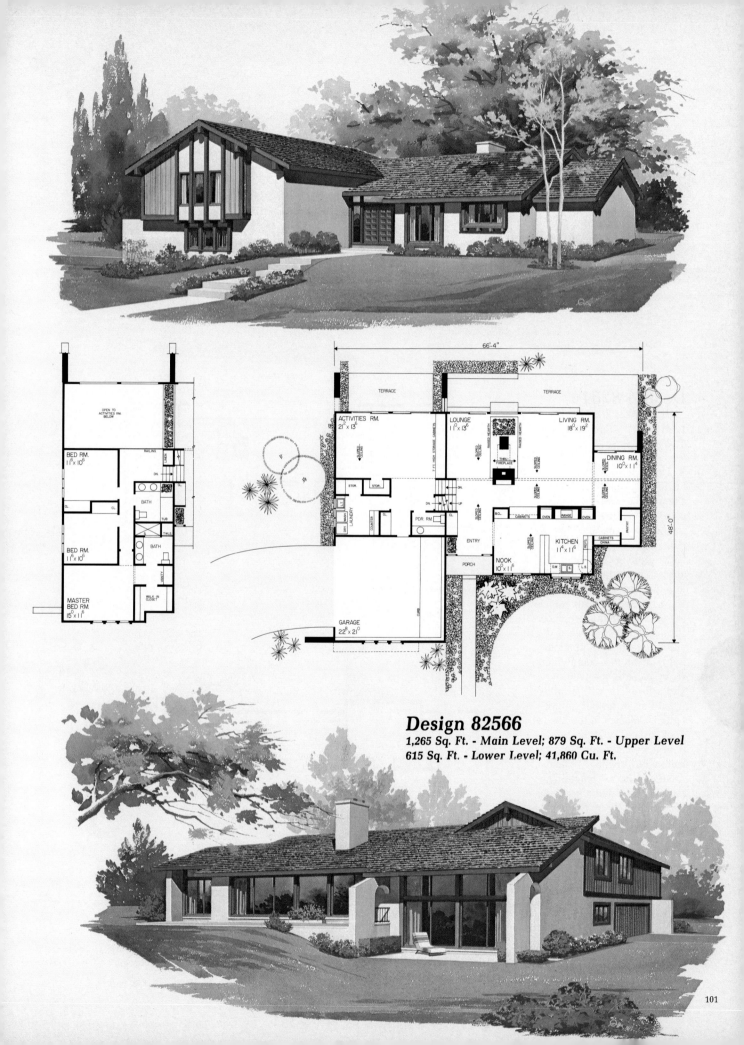

TERRACE

TERRACE

66'-4"

48'-0"

OPEN TO
ACTIVITIES RM.
BELOW

BED RM.
11⁰ x 10⁶

RAILING

LINEN

DN.

CL.

BATH

CL.

CL.

TUB

BED RM.
11⁶ x 10⁶

BATH

VANITY

MASTER
BED RM.
15⁰ x 11⁶

WALK IN
CLOSET

ACTIVITIES RM.
21² x 13⁶

LOUNGE
11⁰ x 13⁶

RAISED HEARTH

RAISED HEARTH

SLOPED CEILING

LIVING RM.
18⁰ x 19²

SLOPED CEILING

THRU-
FIREPLACE

7 FT. HIGH STORAGE CABINETS

DINING RM.
10⁰ x 11⁴

STOR.

STOR.

DN.

UP

B.CL.

CABINETS

OVEN

RANGE

OVEN

LAUNDRY

DRY. WASH.

COUNTER

CL.

PDR. RM.

CL.

ENTRY

KITCHEN
11⁴ x 11⁴

CABINETS

CHINA

PANTRY

REFG.

NOOK
10⁰ x 11⁶

PORCH

D.W.

L.S.

GARAGE
22⁸ x 21⁰

Design 82566
1,265 Sq. Ft. - Main Level; 879 Sq. Ft. - Upper Level
615 Sq. Ft. - Lower Level; 41,860 Cu. Ft.

Design 82614

1,701 Sq. Ft. - First Floor
1,340 Sq. Ft. - Second Floor
31,380 Cu. Ft.

● This one-and-a-half story home has a pleasing appearance with an excellent floor plan. Notice how all the rooms are accessible from a hall. That's a plus for easy housekeeping. This plan includes an exceptionally large family room, more than 20' x 15', which has a beamed ceiling and traditional fireplace. Plus it has a sliding glass door onto the terrace. A gracious living room, too, complemented by paned-glass windows and a fireplace with a built-in wood box. A formal dining room is adjacent to the kitchen/nook area as well. Four large bedrooms including a master suite with private dressing room and bath. Something more! A secluded guest suite, accessible only by the back stairs. You could use it as a spacious library, playroom or a hobby area. Adjacent is a huge storage area or perhaps another room since there are windows at both ends. Note storage area in garage.

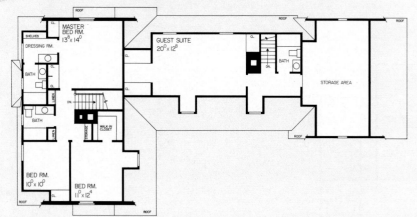

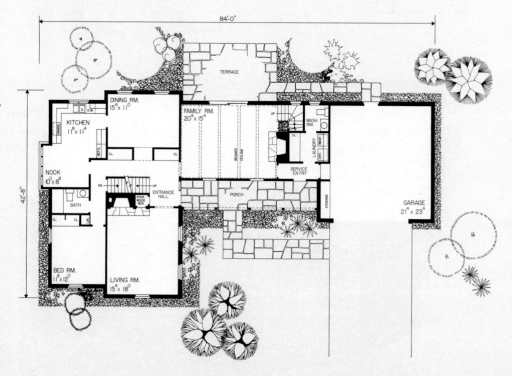

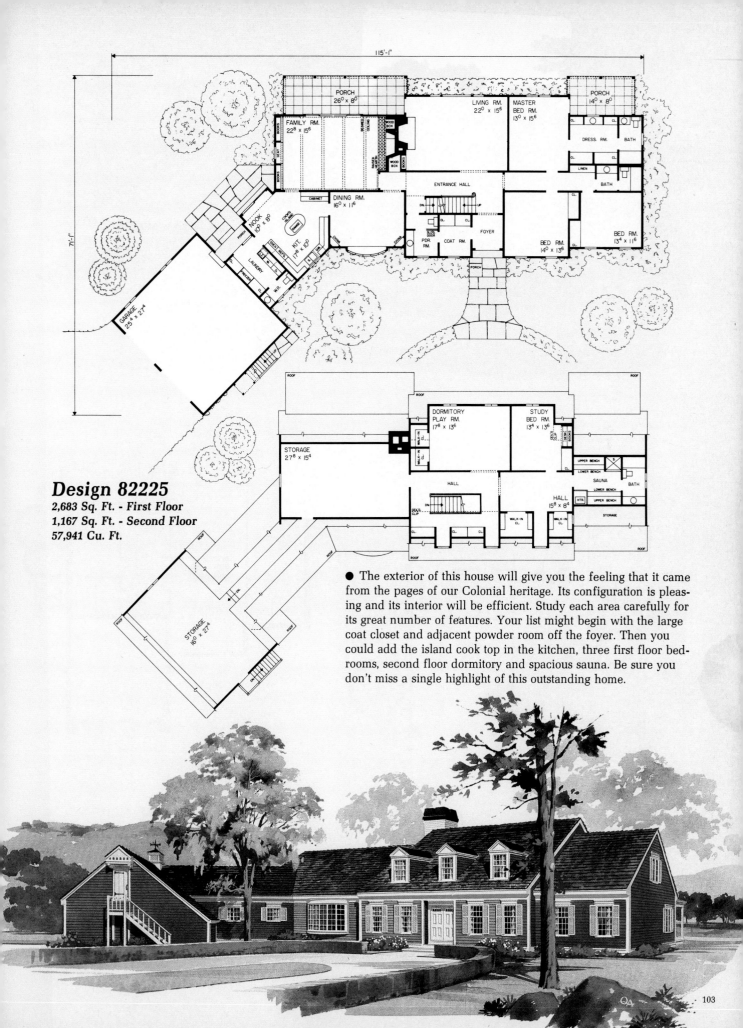

115'-1"

71'-1"

PORCH
26⁰ x 8⁰

FAMILY RM.
22⁸ x 15⁶

LIVING RM.
22⁰ x 15⁶

MASTER
BED RM.
13⁰ x 15⁶

PORCH
14⁰ x 8⁰

DRESS. RM.

BATH

CL

LINEN

BATH

DINING RM.
16⁰ x 11⁶

CABINET

WOOD BOX

ENTRANCE HALL

DN.

UP

FOYER

PDR. RM.

COAT CL.

BED RM.
14⁰ x 13⁶

BED RM.
13⁴ x 11⁶

NOOK
9⁰ x 8⁰

KIT.
17⁸ x 10⁰

LAUNDRY

W.H.

PORCH

GARAGE
25⁴ x 27⁴

ROOF

ROOF

STORAGE
27⁸ x 15⁴

DORMITORY
PLAY RM.
17⁸ x 13⁶

STUDY
BED RM.
13⁴ x 13⁶

HALL

UPPER BENCH

LOWER BENCH

SAUNA

LOWER BENCH

BATH

HALL
15⁸ x 8⁴

HTR.

UPPER BENCH

DN.

WALK-IN CL.

WALK-IN CL.

STORAGE

ROOF

ROOF

STORAGE
16⁰ x 27⁴

ROOF

Design 82225

2,683 Sq. Ft. - First Floor
1,167 Sq. Ft. - Second Floor
57,941 Cu. Ft.

● The exterior of this house will give you the feeling that it came from the pages of our Colonial heritage. Its configuration is pleasing and its interior will be efficient. Study each area carefully for its great number of features. Your list might begin with the large coat closet and adjacent powder room off the foyer. Then you could add the island cook top in the kitchen, three first floor bedrooms, second floor dormitory and spacious sauna. Be sure you don't miss a single highlight of this outstanding home.

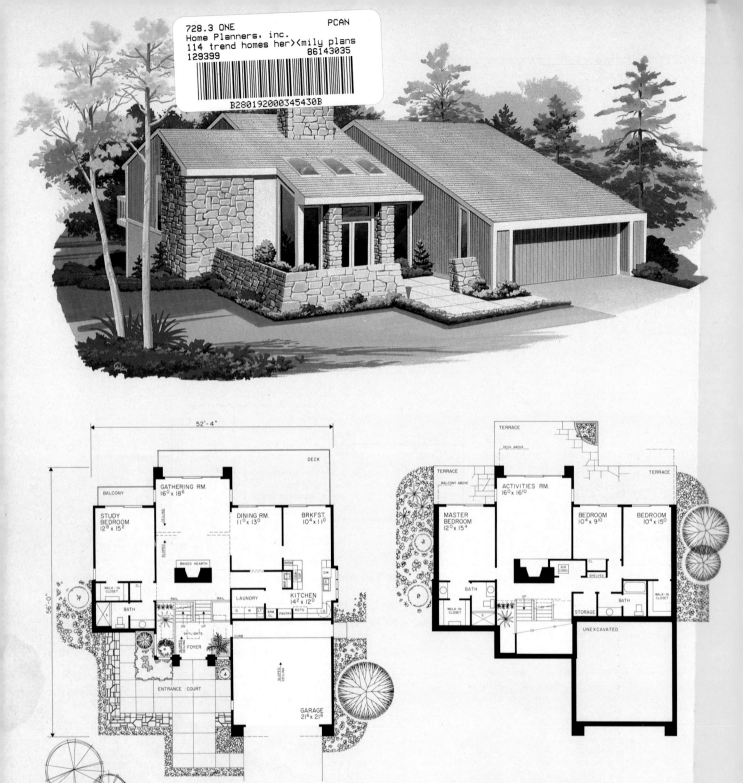

Design 82894
1,490 Sq. Ft. - Main Level
1,357 Sq. Ft. - Lower Level; 38,450 Cu. Ft.

● Contemporary, bi-level living will be enjoyed by all members of the family. Upon entering the foyer, complimented by skylights, stairs will lead you to the upper and lower levels. Up a few steps, you will find yourself in the large gathering room. The fireplace, sloped ceiling and the size of this room will make this a favorite spot. To the left is a study/bedroom with a full bath and walk-in closet. Notice the efficient kitchen and breakfast room with nearby wet bar. The lower level houses two bedrooms and a bath to one side; and a master bedroom suite to the other. Centered is a large activity room with raised-hearth fireplace. It will be enjoyed by all. Note - all of the rear rooms on both levels have easy access to the outdoors for excellent indoor-outdoor livability.